TRUMPING TRUMP

TRUMPING TRUMP

MAKING DEMOCRATICS PROGRESSIVE AGAIN

CONGRESSMAN
BOB FILNER

Copyright © 2017 by Bob Filner

All rights reserved. No part of this book may be used or reproduced in any manner whatsoever without prior written consent of the publisher except in the case of brief quotations embodied in critical articles and reviews. Special book excerpts or customized printings can be created to fit specific needs.

ISBN: 978-0-692-87716-6

Cover and interior design by Dotti Albertine

Printed in the United States of America

*For Erin and Adam, Barbara and Jane—
whose love has always sustained me.*

*In memory of Martin and Robert—
whose lives and deaths have motivated my life.*

CONTENTS

FOREWORD ix

ONE
What Was I Thinking? 1

TWO
Birth of a Progressive 11

THREE
Regaining the Progressive Agenda 29

FOUR
Some Key Progressive Ideas 49

FIVE
Acting Locally: What Does Your Community Need? 61

PHOTOGRAPHS 79

SIX
Fixing the Environment Can Also Fix the Economy 89

SEVEN
Overcoming the Roadblocks to Change 105

EIGHT
Finding Common Ground with the Business Community 123

NINE
Surviving as a Progressive in a Not-So-Progressive World 143

TEN
A Note on Language ... and Law 161

FOREWORD

If you are extremely fortunate, you may experience the more than rare once-in-a-lifetime opportunity to encounter someone who sends you on a journey that leads to places and people you could never imagine knowing. That is the odyssey of Bob Filner as reflected in his analysis of the current Democratic Party.

Under the most unsuspecting circumstances, even in his youth, Bob was privileged to have met the Rev. Dr. Martin Luther King, Jr. who came to his home one evening in search of financial support for his organization while in its infancy. It was Bob's father who found the funds to sustain the Southern Christian Leadership Conference during the terrible, turbulent, and fledging years of building the American Civil Rights movement.

It was that unlikely introduction which propelled Bob into a life-long commitment of nonviolent resistance. Dr. King asked Bob that night to promise that he would never use violence to make much-needed social change. Such a demand placed on the conscience of a 13-year-old Jewish boy in Queens, New York, by a twenty-something black Baptist preacher became seared in his soul and set him on a path. Five years later Bob found himself among the Freedom Riders.

It is sometimes impossible to predict how momentary incidents can transform your life. A casual conversation can possess instructions that when strictly followed can result in decisions that define your purpose. Bob Filner never turned away from Dr. King's handshake and indelible impression of a sacred vow not to use destructive tactics that harm human life.

Dating back to that private encounter with Dr. King as a child carried Bob through his early years of maturing and enduring the cruel backlash of racial injustice and discrimination. Such a long held tradition throughout the South put him in contact with white supremacist thugs who beat him up and threw him in jail for a cause in which many lesser persons refused to participate.

Reading Bob's story and learning about his steady steps into public life as the President of the San Diego, California, School Board to ten terms in the United States Congress is a course in courage and savvy observation of political systems at the local and national levels.

Perhaps nothing happens by accident. Maybe there is a predestination of events that mark a person for incredible responsibilities. Whatever the means by which he was projected onto the stage of public service, Bob found the way to use his position to influence legislation that benefitted his constituents.

Although he was an outspoken opponent of war, Bob fought to provide much needed health coverage for veterans who returned home but who were without access to the care they deserved after suffering post-traumatic stress disorder (PTSD). He was a strong advocate for veterans' housing as the bane of homelessness spread and increased, leaving too many of them on the streets across the United States without any place to live.

Bob Filner's story is about an imperfect, flawed, and completely human person who found himself in the glaring spotlight of public scrutiny at a time when his political career was surging upward. After serving more than two decades in Congress, he returned to San Diego and was elected mayor in his adopted hometown.

An inglorious fall from grace put him on yet another path, which required deep soul searching and high profiled agony. Bob was forced to face demons that lurked within, among, and around him. He did not escape their clutches.

Marred by personal imperfections, he was forced to delve into the depths of self-assessment that required extraordinary recovery and renewal in order to reclaim his life.

This book is more than a tale of diverse episodes that defined his way forward from a university professor who became a proponent of quality education for all children in the public system. He recalls more than his meteoric flight to the highest echelons of government under the guidance of

Senator Hubert Humphrey and Congressmembers Andrew Young (later Mayor of Atlanta) and Don Fraser (later Mayor of Minneapolis).

Bob shares the critical lessons he learned along the way. He uses his past as a roadmap to encourage others who dare take a bolder direction. He invites us to correct the ills that haunt our nation.

This book is a primer for anyone who wants to know how to effectively organize a community and take action to gain access to the halls of power. Congressman Filner offers the gift of his wisdom and experience to inspire his readers to stand up, step out, and speak truth to power without fear, shame, or apology.

—Rev. Dr. Art Cribbs, Executive Director,
Interfaith Movement for Human Integrity

ONE

What Was I Thinking?

Only those who dare to fail greatly can ever achieve greatly.
—Robert F. Kennedy

What I remember most about the guy on the train to Los Angeles was the redness of his face. His anger flushed his cheeks to the point I thought his face might bleed, and he wouldn't stop staring at me from across the aisle. I kept my eyes on my paper and tried to ignore him. It hummed in my brain that, at any moment, he was going to jump out of his seat and smack me in the head.

Not that I didn't deserve such an act of hostility; I probably did. A little retribution for all that I had lost and given away. For all those I had hurt.

I ignored him. Today I was minding my own business, just Citizen Bob for the first time in thirty years, trying to get somewhere on the 5:30 p.m. train. I knew what he wanted to say. I had been hearing those words everywhere for the past year, ever since resigning as the mayor of San Diego—I was a jerk, a misogynist, an abuser, a sexual pervert. I had messed up, sure I had, but I knew I wasn't any of those things. Who was I, then? I had asked myself that often lately. I was a man who needed to confront his demons, pay his dues, and change. A man who did change.

The guy next to me stood in the aisle, the train gently rocking, I held my breath. "You're Filner, aren't you?"

I looked up at him. Boy, was he tall.

"Yeah, I'm Bob Filner."

I had met many, many angry constituents over the years, and I'd always listened to them. I had done that for thirty years: listened to people, to their troubles and to their needs. That was how I got things done. If this guy was about to hit me, I wanted to look him in the eye. I stood and we faced each other.

"I just wanted you to know that I always supported you. I can forgive you for all that stupid stuff you did."

Now this was disarming. I started to relax a bit.

"But I'll never forget what you did," he added. "You set the movement back ten years." He wasn't smiling when he said that.

Yeah, in addition to hurting a lot of people, that's what I had done. I could see it and hear it in this man—he had lost something.

What Was I Thinking?

There had been those moments of bright hope that things could really change in San Diego, that it could become something better than it had ever been. We didn't have to live in the past, beholden to the power elite and their "good old boy" way of doing business. As great as this city is, it could be an even greater place to live and work. But my stupid behavior had given our enemies the chance to run in and tear it all down. That was a good reason to be mad.

I have spent the last four years of my life in emotional exile, examining the very things this man was so angry about. What was it in my life that allowed me to get off track? How had my own behavior derailed not only my own career, but the hopes and aspirations of so many who had elected me—like the fellow on the train? I had let him and a lot of other regular folks down. After plenty of reflection (and three months of house arrest), I knew I needed to change many things.

I don't have a problem with change. My thirty years of public service were built on change. I believed that if people were involved in their own communities, if they had a voice in how a city or neighborhood was run—and if it wasn't always up to the fat cats and power brokers to call all the shots—they could have better lives. Their children would be safer and they could get the things every American has come to expect as part of the American Dream. They didn't need to feel disenfranchised in their own country.

It's possible to have a responsive government that serves all of the neighborhoods—not just the rich ones, not just the white ones, not just the ones where the major campaign contributors live. When regular people begin to see that they can make a difference and have a say in how their city is operated, hope blossoms.

I tested these beliefs in 1987 in Sherman Heights, a rough little neighborhood squeezed in between downtown and the suburbs. I was a Democrat trying to win a seat on a City Council dominated by Republicans. I knew Democrats had trouble winning, so I took my campaign to this forgotten neighborhood. Sherman Heights was a place where clutches of immigrant families often settled and established themselves before moving on. The first year I ran for City Council, many African Americans and Latinos lived there.

I went door-to-door introducing myself. I began by asking them about their concerns. The mothers told me about the busy streets, cars racing from downtown to the suburbs, whipping by all day. Their kids had to cross these roadways twice a day to get to school and back. At every door I knocked on, I heard the same thing. They wanted a stop sign on this busy boulevard.

I asked them, "Why don't you go to City Hall?" They said they had, but no one had listened because they only spoke Spanish.

I knew the City Council well. The council of nine had a majority of conservatives, but I knew they had a committee—consisting of three Democrats and two Republicans—that actually could make decisions about stop signs. I gathered the parents of Sherman Heights and told them we had to go to this committee meeting and tell their story. I told them not to worry about the language barrier, because I'd see that everything was translated.

They came in force and told their stories about how unsafe

it was for their kids to cross the busy streets. Sure enough, the committee voted three to two, just as I thought they would, to install a stop sign. The families were ecstatic. Because of the committee's actions, we were able to install four stop signs on the busy street that bisected their neighborhood.

I wanted to do something special to celebrate the stop signs and to show the entire neighborhood that they really had a voice. We put paper bags over the new stop signs, and I gathered the entire community—more than a thousand people, including about 600 school children—on one corner in Sherman Heights, to wait for the unveiling. I gave a little speech about how it was *their* voice that had been heard. I reminded them never to forget the power they had. And they used this victory to build true community power!

That was my first taste of community organizing, and I've never forgotten it. After I was elected, I went from community to community planting stop signs. We had celebrations and picnics together. I ate with them, and laughed with them, and I worked hard for them.

As a city councilman, I formed action groups in my district. I taught people how to assess their community's concerns. The next item on the Sherman Heights list was the schoolyard playground. A helicopter ride over the city, beginning in the north, would reveal large patches of green in all the school yards—but as you flew farther south, the school yards were all brown. Not even brown grass; just dirt.

I asked the residents what they wanted, and they said they wanted grass like the other neighborhoods had. I told them they needed to bring their community groups and come to city hall and demand grass for their fields. They did that, and we beautified every field in the district.

The citizen groups eventually became self-sustaining. They gathered on their own and learned how to address their concerns. They still operate today. My life may be marked by disgrace and shame, but I'm still very proud of what we accomplished in Sherman Heights and many other neighborhoods.

All those years I represented that district, I attended school graduations. I even handed out diplomas and shook hands with the graduates to congratulate them on their achievements. I attended their barbecues, and dances. They didn't care if I was liberal or conservative or white or whatever. They knew I would stand with them to get things done to better their communities. They'd helped me get elected, and I showed them what a government that works for them could accomplish.

I knew that, if I spent enough time with people, I could understand their problems and help them. That's what elected officials are supposed to do—listen to their constituents and advocate on their behalf. One of the things I did was work with the city contracting department, making sure minority contractors got their fair share of city work, which wasn't always the case before I took my seat on the council. It was a dogfight getting the policies changed, but we got it done. I tried to make city contracting for goods and services fair and open to everyone, no matter the size of the company.

After five years on the City Council, I took my agenda of change to a larger stage. In 1992, I was elected to the U.S. House of Representatives from the 51st Congressional

What Was I Thinking?

District—a district that was 85 percent people of color, with the largest single population of Filipinos in the country. For twenty years, I represented their interests, and they reelected me nine times. One of the Washington legacies I'm most proud of is my role as an early member of the Congressional Progressive Caucus. The caucus still operates today, advocating on behalf of those whose voices are seldom heard.

I came home full of hope that it was time for San Diego to assert itself as one of America's premier cities. When I ran for Mayor in 2012, no Democrat had been elected in twenty years. That didn't bother me at all. I knew nearly every neighborhood in the city. After we won, I came into office under full sail. I had more than a hundred items on my to-do list. Why should these things take years and years to get done?

My plan was to rally folks around me and get results. The more I talked about the innovative things we wanted to do, the more the excitement in the people around me grew. What I didn't anticipate—maybe due to my own naiveté—was the provincial backlash from the status quo.

I had a plan to get all the homeless veterans off the street. We'd be the first major city in America to accomplish this. It's a social travesty and a black mark on our city's character that San Diego is known as the home of one of the largest navy fleets in the world, while homeless soldiers and sailors roam our streets, panhandling for their meals.

We had a bus-pass program designed to help poor children get to school. We had a climate action plan. I proposed that San Diego should co-host the world's first bi-national Olympics with Tijuana. We also talked about the feasibility of installing solar panels on all the public buildings and schools in the city. To date, no city in America has done that.

The agenda for our first year was ambitious. Looking back, I know it was too ambitious. I didn't prioritize the most feasible and important projects and put the rest on the long-term agenda. We had a vision of a city that would be progressive in its policies and friendly to all its citizens—and as exciting as that was for many, it also scared some people in the halls of power.

Soon enough, I was fighting a three-front war—with the city attorney, the business community, and the City Council. I had no idea the backlash would be so personal. When the allegations of sexual harassment and abuse first surfaced, I was in such denial that I dismissed them in my mind as part of a strategy to bring all my initiatives to a standstill. My mind was on all the projects we had in the works: the application for the 2024 Olympics, the solar conversion of the city buildings, and so much more.

Everything changed when my communications director resigned and filed a lawsuit claiming sexual harassment.

Then the "lynch mob" (a term used by one of my children) surfaced, and woman after woman came out of my past, telling story after story. These accusations hit me like a baseball bat to the head. I'd truly had no idea they'd found my actions offensive. I was forced to reexamine my past behavior.

When I looked within myself, I confronted a monster. I even said that to a TV reporter: "I brought this on myself through my own personal frailties, and the biggest monster right now is inside me." A short time later, while I was still mayor, I went into "rehab."

In the months since my resignation as mayor of San Diego, with the help of professionals who specialized in my issues, I've come to some deep conclusions about myself. I had picked up a bad habit while in office, one I truly didn't have when I ran that first campaign for City Council so many years before. My years in office had made me arrogant and drunk with power—and I'm deeply ashamed of that. I thought my power and my position exempted me from the rules and boundaries others had to observe. I never stole money, but I did abuse my power as an elected official to convince women to sleep with me. My arrogance blinded me to the demeaning way I had treated women.

I was having casual relationships and thinking it was just one of the perks of office. I always assumed these encounters were consensual. My "success" with women made me even more arrogant. I began to think that, wherever I went, women would want to sleep with me. They would want to be close to my power.

But I've learned that, when you have power, these relationships are rarely equal. The women felt pressured, even though they didn't tell me that. They never complained, so I never stopped. Everything had seemed consensual to me. Now I know that I was wrong.

My behavior became addictive, meaning I had to have more and more conquests. Now I can see that it wasn't the sex I was after; it was the power. And the abuse of that power led to my downfall. My resignation in disgrace put an end to everything I had done in good faith, for the benefit of all the people of San Diego.

It has taken me a while to think about that guy on the train. He could forgive me for my weaknesses, and how I'd let them rule me and control my behavior. What he couldn't forgive me for was the fact that everything we had begun to build in the city with my election as mayor had come to a complete standstill.

I have two things to say to the man on the train, and to every person like him who has a vision of a better mayor and a better America. First, my addiction is not gone. I will have to live with the regret of what I've done for the rest of my life. But I have changed my behavior. I'm learning to treat women and others around me with humility and grace. I will work on this for the rest of my days.

Second, the vision of a Progressive America is far from dead. Our communities can be places of equality and justice for everyone—black, white, brown, yellow, gay, straight, men and women—and even Bob Filner.

I have a lot to say about how America can change for the better. Stay with me through the following pages—we have a lot of battles to fight.

TWO

Birth of a Progressive

The ultimate measure of a man is not where he stands in moments of convenience and comfort, but where he stands at times of challenge and controversy.
—Dr. Martin Luther King, Jr., 1963

I never planned to run for public office. For much of my early life, I believed that the best way to change a political system that discriminated against its own citizens was from the outside, through non-violent civil action. My father had drilled into me his way of seeing the world: that by the time people were elected to office, they had been bought and sold so many times that they hardly could remember what they believed. The system itself had become corrupted, and only pressure from citizen agitators would force changes in our institutions that would grant equal justice and opportunity for *all* Americans.

My social values were formed early, influenced by an activist father who took part in some of the great events that shaped his times. His experiences rubbed off on me in myriad ways.

Meeting Dr. King

I must have been about thirteen that day I came home from school and found a group of black men sitting at our kitchen table. My father introduced me to these men, including Bayard Rustin and Dr. Martin Luther King, Jr. To this day, what I remember most about Dr. King is his strength and gentleness when I shook his hand. I didn't know much about him except what my father had told me—that he would be a great man who would do incredible things for our nation. My father was an early financial supporter of Dr. King and a believer in Dr. King's strategy for effecting change through non-violent civil agitation.

That day in our kitchen, Dr. King asked me if I wanted to join the fight for justice and equality. I said I did, and he made me swear to non-violence for the rest of my life. Of course, I hardly understood the implications of this little ceremony at the time, but it nonetheless had a marked influence on my thinking from that point on.

To my father, this wasn't a trite little ritual; rather, it was an important moment in his lifetime of effort to seek a more equal society for the marginalized and oppressed. My father's story begins in the thirties, during the Depression, when he was working as a union organizer on the front line with the steelworkers and teamsters, seeking better pay and working conditions. Like many young Americans, he joined the Army after Pearl Harbor. He believed in fighting for freedom, and he saw fascism as a palpable threat to everything all Americans stood for.

Late in the war, he was with his unit in Italy chasing fascists up the boot when the call went out for soldiers who could speak Yiddish. He was transferred to the front lines with Patton's Third Army, where he was among the first group of men to reach Dachau, near Munich. To say he was horrified by what he saw would be an understatement.

He was tasked with translating the debriefing of concentration camp prisoners for American intelligence. He heard their stories first-hand. He saw, up close, how inhumanity had been fashioned into a national policy. He witnessed the tragedy of the destruction of his people—my people. He felt the hatred of a whole nation for the Jewish people ... just for being Jewish.

That's when his letters to me began. I was only two years old at the time, but I kept them and read them often in the years that followed. Besides describing what he had seen, he urged me to remember that if this unthinkable genocide could happen in one of the most civilized nations on earth, it could happen to Jews in America someday, too.

My father came home from the war with a deeper understanding of the fragility of democracy. He was more determined than ever to stand with anyone who fought for equality and justice. America promised equal opportunity for everyone, regardless of race or religion, but large groups of people—minorities, women, and others—had been left far behind. Equality was something worth fighting for.

In the 1950s, my father was attracted to Dr. King's message of peaceful civil action. He saw King's organizing skills and non-violent methods as a way to exert pressure on democratic institutions. My father's passion and dedication influenced me, so when the call went out in the late spring of 1961 for volunteers to join the Freedom Riders on a bus ride through the deeply segregated South, I didn't hesitate. After spending the summer in the Mississippi State Penitentiary with my fellow Freedom Riders for doing nothing more than riding on an integrated bus, I knew I would be involved in social action for the rest of my life.

I moved west to California after obtaining my doctorate in history and I took up teaching at San Diego State. I intended to establish my teaching career and find my way into activism.

A Year in Washington, D.C.

After a couple of years of wrestling with the demands of the education system, I came to the realization that I wasn't very good at teaching. Looking back, I now understand that I didn't struggle in the classroom because I lacked knowledge of my subject; I knew my material cold. But it takes more than knowledge to teach—it takes a passion that inspires students to open themselves up to new ideas.

Whatever it was I lacked, I knew I needed a leave of absence. So in 1975, I applied for, and was granted, a one-year Congressional Fellowship to work on Capitol Hill. I worked for six months as an aide to Senator Hubert Humphrey and then spent another six months working for Congressman Dan Fraser.

It was during my time with Senator Humphrey that I came to understand the full impact a national lawmaker could have on national policy. I learned that this job of legislating takes energy and a willingness to exert effort to reach your goals. It also takes daring, which arises from deeply held beliefs. That's what my father had. That's what Dr. King had. Senator Humphrey had it in spades. He was a whirlwind of ideas that, if enacted, would have used the government to solve our problems in the areas of full employment, health care, civil rights, technology, and rural development, among other issues.

Senator Humphrey was forward-thinking and he understood that technology would change the face of our nation, including what kinds of jobs would be available, how we grew food, and how health care was delivered. He was one of the founding board members of the Office of Technological Assessment (OTA), a non-partisan, bicameral Congressional committee that tapped the best scientific minds of our nation to investigate trends affecting the country's growth and health. I worked closely with him on many of the issues the panel took up. The OTA issued non-partisan reports that were scientifically accurate and useful in developing legislation and national policy to prepare for the future.

The OTA is defunct now, thanks to Newt Gingrich and his party's shortsightedness. Gingrich's so-called "Contract with America," enacted in 1994, and his penurious way of gutting government entities for purely ideological reasons made no sense at all. Closing down such a useful panel of experts saved taxpayers $25 million a year—but no one talks about what it cost us not to have one credible body to evaluate technology. These evaluations have been moved to outside foundations and research bodies. None of these are truly neutral, and most of their research reports come to legislators in the hands of lobbyists with an agenda to promote.

If there is one thing Washington doesn't need, it's more lobbyists promoting scientific breakthroughs to further the interests of their clients. The Republicans' approach to technology is the same approach they take to almost every issue—they mostly seek the benefit of their wealthy patrons, who have purchased their tickets to sit in Congress. To place our nation's scientific development primarily in the hands of lobbyists puts more power in the hands of fewer and fewer people.

Humphrey's work on the OTA was symptomatic of his approach to government. If government had the best available knowledge at its disposal, he believed, legislators could make rational choices that were best for the nation as a whole. One of his biographers observed that, "Humphrey more or less invented the modern senator, as we now know him ... creator, educator, innovator, using his place and prominence to define issues for the broader public—and ultimately, through mastery of the interminable process of committee, cloakroom, and floor maneuver, translating these issues into law."[1]

---

1. Iric Nathanson, "The Final Chapter: Hubert Humphrey Returns to Public Life," *MinnPost*, May 26, 2011, www.minnpost.com/politics-policy/2011/05/final-chapter-hubert-humphrey-returns-public-life, quoted in Carl Solberg, *Hubert Humphrey: A Biography* (St. Paul, MN: Borealis Book, 2004).

This is exactly how Humphrey operated. As a young post-doctoral intern trying to find my way, I was impressed with how and why he worked so hard. In my mind, he was a force for radical change, and it was a rare opportunity for me to see how change could be shaped from inside the system—something my father thought wasn't possible.

I also learned about myself and what I was capable of. I have many memories of working alongside him, but one stands out—despite its seeming triviality—for what it did for my confidence. One evening, the Senator and I entered a ballroom in a Washington hotel where he was scheduled to speak. On the drive over, we talked over issues and details that needed attention. It wasn't until we were in the hotel lobby among the other guests that he stopped cold and said, "I can't go in there." I asked him why not. "Look, everyone's in tuxes." And it was true; he wasn't dressed appropriately. Evidently, whoever scheduled the speech hadn't communicated the black-tie dress requirements. Dress formalities in Washington were strictly observed.

Trying to figure out what to do, I looked around the room. Coming out of the dining rooms, I noticed the waiters were well-dressed in formal attire for the evening. One of them appeared to be about Senator Humphrey's size, so I approached him. I explained our problem to him, and he agreed to an exchange. We ducked into a nearby bathroom and made the quick change-over, and the senator went on to the dinner and gave his speech.

The next day when I showed up at the Senator's office for work, the whole staff stood and applauded me. I can't say it was a watershed moment in my life, but it did convince me I had the presence of mind to survive under pressure. After that, I shouldered more responsibility, took on more challenging tasks, and returned to San Diego more confident and focused.

My classroom back at San Diego State now seemed much smaller and less intimidating. I went about my work as a professor of history, but I wasn't the same person. My students and my department head noticed the changes.

I was ready for new challenges.

Working for Change

My family grew, and my two children began attending our neighborhood elementary school. In 1978, I was elected president of the PTA. One of the responsibilities of the position was to meet monthly with the school principal to discuss parental concerns. During one meeting, we were struggling with a difficult issue—what it was, I don't remember—when the principal said we didn't have to worry about it because the school would be closing at the end of the year.

"What?" I asked. "When was this decided?"

"A couple of years ago," she said, a little surprised I didn't know.

"Who decided this?"

"The school board."

She went on to tell me how they had decided to close ten schools across the city to save money. I asked her when the board met.

"Tuesday afternoons at two."

That figured. They met at a time when most parents couldn't attend. But they hadn't counted on a professor who taught classes on Mondays, Wednesdays, and Fridays! So I went to my first school board meeting.

During the public comment time, I asked about the school closings, explaining that my children's school would be affected by their decision. I expected a civil discussion. Instead, the response from the school board was hostile and patronizing. They couldn't believe I was wasting their time questioning their decision. Then I was told my three minutes were up and I needed to take my seat.

I sat in the audience and seethed. They hadn't answered any of my questions! Instead, they had treated me like I had no right to challenge their decision. This was an imperial board. I was shocked and surprised that these people could do virtually as they pleased, and that they thought they could cow residents into accepting their edicts.

I began attending meetings regularly and discovered my experience wasn't unique. They treated anyone who questioned their authority in the same imperious way.

That's when I decided I had seen enough.

I went to each of the affected schools, spoke before their PTAs, and announced that I was organizing a citywide Committee Against School Closures. The committee consisted of parents from each of the schools. We went to work researching how the closures had come about and studying the board's justification. We also researched the facts about the schools—attendance, growth, funding, etc. We had every statistic imaginable available to us. I thought we had a good case. Now we needed to present our findings.

We began to show up at school board meetings—sometimes several hundred of us (which completely filled up the meeting auditorium!). Contrary to the board's claims about shrinking enrollment, we showed that the district wasn't shrinking; it was expanding. We showed how the closures would adversely affect schools across the city. We made presentations at every meeting until the board finally relented and put the closures to a new vote. This time, the board voted to keep every one of the schools open. We had won!

In the excitement of the moment, one of the committee members said I should run for a spot on the school board. They said I knew as much about running a school district as anyone currently serving on the board.

I had volunteered during several electoral campaigns, so I knew the toll they took on a person. I also knew you needed financial backing. I had nothing—no organization, no financial backers, only my desire to make a difference.

I decided to run on a "Back to Basics" platform. The board elections began with a primary that selected the top two candidates from each district. Those candidates would then face off in a citywide election. I knew the system was designed to keep Democrats out of office, since San Diego was heavily Republican.

Mine was a shoe-leather campaign. For months, I spent every day walking door to door in my district. I knocked on thousands of doors. Then I sent a follow-up letter to each person I had spoken to, thanking them for their time and mentioning the issue we had discussed.

In the primary, the incumbent won 60 percent of the votes and I won 40 percent. Against all the odds, I had made the runoff, but I didn't think I had a chance to go further. I was still a complete unknown. A Democrat had never defeated an incumbent Republican for *any* office in San Diego. I was exhausted after working twelve-hour days knocking on doors for months, and that was in one small district. How could I reach the entire city in only six weeks?

It was during our first debate that I discovered I *did* have a chance. That election included every city position from mayor down to the school board. The debate included all thirty-six candidates, and I was the last one to speak. By the time I came to the podium, the auditorium was nearly empty. I had just begun to speak about my platform when I noticed that a newspaper reporter who had been introduced to me earlier in the evening was still in the audience.

My opponent, who had spoken right before me, had advocated defying the Civil Rights Act, which required black teachers to be assigned district-wide instead of just to lower-income black schools. Her reason for defying the law—that black kids needed role models—was sound, but she was still advocating defiance of one of the nation's most sweeping reforms. I pointed at the reporter and said, "And you should write in your newspaper that this incumbent advocates defying our nation's civil rights laws."

I learned that night that, if you supply reporters with good kindling, they will find a way to light a bonfire. The next day, he wrote a scathing article about my opponent's statement advocating defiance of the Civil Rights Act. I began getting calls—the first was from a radio station. I did my first radio interview over the phone. I was astonished at how easy it was. So I called all the radio stations in the city and gave interviews. Soon, I was being invited to speak all over San Diego.

The relationships I had built while organizing against the school closures helped me significantly. Since I had no election committee or other help, I organized around the elementary schools in the city. I spoke at parent gatherings whenever I could. I put in many hours getting my message out: *every* child deserves a quality education.

It ended up being a very close election. I won my seat with just 50.4 percent of the vote. I was exhausted, but exhilarated. That I could win a citywide election beginning with almost zero name recognition surprised even me. But I had done it. And two years later, I was elected President of the Board!

I count among my proudest achievements hiring one of the finest school superintendents the city has ever had. I and other board members had become dissatisfied with the superintendent we inherited. He used his position to run a petty fiefdom instead of focusing energy and resources on the education of our children. After we were able to terminate him, we hired Dr. Tom Payzant, who worked hard for our district for the next decade before heading off to Washington, D.C. to work in President Clinton's Department of Education. I'm very proud of what we accomplished together during Payzant's tenure.

One thing I had learned working for Hubert Humphrey was that if we want to experience the full extent of our freedoms, we have to engage in the process. "Freedom is hammered out on the anvil of discussion, dissent, and debate," Humphrey said in one of his speeches. Freedom doesn't just happen; it is won through effort and sacrifice and determination.

I believe one of the first requirements for true freedom is the opportunity to receive a quality education. Education opens doors. Lack of quality education keeps people impoverished by limiting their opportunities. Education is the bedrock of a truly equal society. That's why I felt so strongly that the schools in minority and ethnic neighborhoods needed to be every bit as competently run as the schools in wealthy La Jolla.

After winning a seat on the city council and working as a councilman and deputy mayor for five years, I decided to run for a national office, representing the 50th Congressional District. It was a big step, but one for which I'd prepared for many years. I wanted to be an effective radical from within.

Thirty Days to Live

I hadn't been in Congress long when a woman named Evelyn came into my office. She looked at least seventy years old. When she told me she was only fifty, I had a hard time believing her. She had a strained look to her, as if something deadly was pulling at her from the inside. I asked her what I could do for her.

"I need your help," she said. "I only have thirty days to live, and I need an operation."

She told me her frustrating tale of trying to get her insurance company and Medicare to communicate with each other to approve her operation. She needed a rare and dangerous triple organ transplant, and she needed it soon; without it, her doctor had told her, she would die.

The issue wasn't the availability of the organs. She had found a doctor who could help her, and the organs were available. The problem was her insurance. She had a private policy and Medicare, and neither one of them could agree on who would pay for what, so they just stalled her. Medicare had told her that, since she had private insurance, they couldn't help her. The private insurance said they were secondary to Medicare.

It sounded to me as if both insurers were just waiting out the time until they didn't have to spend any money on her. She had spent two agonizing months of her life arguing with these bureaucracies. By the time she came to me, her life clock was ticking down, and she was desperate.

I didn't have the power to tell anyone what to do. The only power I possessed was my title as U.S. Congressman: When I called, people picked up the phone. I had found I could use that power effectively on behalf of my constituents.

When I was first elected to the House, I didn't understand how I could be effective at helping individuals. Rather, I envisioned myself walking into the halls of power and shaking things up on a large scale. I wasn't certain how I would go about accomplishing my goals from the inside, but I didn't think I would do it one person at a time—until this lady walked into my office. In Congress, they call individual problems taken up by legislators "casework." Shortly after I won my first term in the House, I realized that successful casework would do many things for me as a congressman.

To stay in power, I had to get reelected every two years. Helping my constituents obviously makes campaigning easier. People in my district knew they had my ear if they needed me.

I also learned how powerful successful problem-solving could be. I didn't let anyone leave my office without asking myself and my staff, "What's the next step?"

That's what I did that day when the lady with thirty days to live told me her problem. I sat her down and told her, "Okay, Evelyn, you're not leaving here until we solve this problem."

I got Medicare on the phone and explained her situation. The finger pointing began right away, so I asked them to hold on. I got her private insurance company on another line. Then I made them talk to one another. I wouldn't let them off the phone until we had a solution. They decided to split the costs 60/40. I don't remember who paid what, but I do remember seeing the woman again a couple of months later, after she'd had the surgery. This time she looked her age—a healthy, vibrant fifty-year-old. I couldn't believe the change. *I had helped save her life!*

It seems odd that as a congressman I would have to intervene in such a personal way to get her the help she needed. But during my years in office, I discovered that not only was this the most satisfying part of my job as a representative, but it was also instrumental in helping me understand the ways in which the system wasn't working for the people in my district.

Casework was every bit as important as working on the big issues in Washington. Over time, I became known for getting issues resolved for my constituents. This practical problem-solving skill became the leverage that kept my reelection campaigns rolling, term after term. You don't have to work too hard to convince the locals to vote for you if they already know you as the go-to-person to untangle a visa problem, an intractable insurance company that won't pay out benefits, or some other pressing issue. I never counted the exact number of times that I was able to help individuals over the years—but it had to be in the tens of thousands.

In reality, a congressman has little power to change things except by the work he or she performs in his or her home district. Most major legislation is proposed and controlled by the House leaders, so casework was where I believed I could make my mark as a congressman. I assigned half my staff to the district office in San Diego, and I always took a personal interest in solving problems. I didn't allow cases to go unresolved unless they were truly unresolvable, and that only happened in rare instances.

Another reason I wanted to get personally involved was that I wanted to understand the problems people faced. I wanted to see up close the obstacles they encountered. From observing these situations, I developed my most important legislative ideas. I worked many of these ideas into laws that benefited working-class people across the nation.

As much as I enjoyed casework, I didn't think this was how I would always use my time as a congressman—assisting someone to get an organ transplant or working with a group of Filipino veterans to ensure that they received retirement benefits that had been promised to them, or building parks and sidewalks.

One person's illness or one person's visa problem are microcosmic examples of how government can work for people if they have a voice. In a representative government, someone has to do the representing when the people need it. I used every bit of the power I had as a congressman to fill that role as a representative of the people.

In the greater macro-sphere of issues facing our nation, I had spent considerable time in Congress trying to work a progressive agenda into national legislation. I helped organize the Progressive Caucus in the House during my first term, to gather like-minded progressives into a cohesive force. Although we continued to meet throughout my term in the House, it didn't take long to realize that legislative power is held securely in the hands of the party leadership. The possibility of radical changes in key issues that are important to progressives is bound up in an arcane process—hemmed in by rules and controlled by powerful congressmen who are heavily influenced by persuasive, well-financed special-interest groups.

When the opportunity arose for me to come home to San Diego and run for mayor, I jumped at the chance. In 2012, after a hard-fought campaign, I was sworn in as the first Democratic mayor of San Diego in a generation.

I came into office with a vision of remaking San Diego into a showplace of progressive innovation. Even though it's the eighth-largest city in America, San Diego still had a provincial view of itself. Armed with a list of one hundred things I wanted to accomplish, I set to work. My vision would transform San Diego into a more inclusive city that would provide greater opportunity for every neighborhood.

However, I let my personal weaknesses stymie my plans. I disappointed not only myself, but also those who had believed in me. I deeply regret my failings, not only because of the personal shame they have brought me, but even more so, because of the work I left undone. It's that work I spent thirty years pursuing—and the work I left undone—that I want to talk about in this book.

THREE

Regaining the Progressive Agenda

Make a career of humanity. Commit yourself to the noble struggle for equal rights. You will make a better person of yourself, a greater nation of your country, and a finer world to live in.
— Dr. Martin Luther King, Jr.

I don't remember where I was that April day in 2014 when it broke in the national press that thirty-five veterans had died in Phoenix while waiting for appointments to see a physician. Fake appointments had been made in the logs, so administrators could report that they had met department service goals. Meanwhile, the vets had died waiting to get medical care.

I felt more than shocked. I felt revulsion, and maybe a tinge of shame for my country, to think that men and women who had sacrificed so much had been treated so shabbily by the very institution designed to help them. I knew our government could do better—much better. I also knew what would happen to those who had caused this tragedy for our veterans.

Nothing.

I believe that government on all levels—local, state, and federal—can do better for the people it claims to serve. It has to do better.

Freedom is something that Americans take great pride in. But what is freedom without adequate healthcare, without the benefits you've earned, without access to quality education, or a job with a decent wage, or enough to eat, or the civil liberties we are all promised, or a safe neighborhood to live in? What kind of freedom is that? It can't be freedom for the few, or we'll fall back into a feudal society. It has to be freedom for all of us.

I've spent my political career championing progressive ideals, first in local government (on the San Diego School Board and City Council), and then in Congress for twenty years. Unfortunately, I've watched the tide of progressivism—and the changes it can bring to the American people—recede into ineffectiveness. I believe a revived Progressive Movement will rekindle the hope many Americans have for a better future.

The benefits won by progressives are so commonplace now in our daily lives that we forget where they came from. It was the Progressive Movement that extended civil rights and labor protections to every American. The movement was responsible for women's suffrage, direct election of U.S. Senators, anti-trust legislation, child labor protections, the eight-hour workday, and more. In the 1950s and '60s, the Progressive Movement fought to end segregation and eradicate Jim Crow laws.

But that energy to fight for revolutionary changes seemingly has dissipated, melted away into a comfortable status quo. Yes, we have seen an Occupy movement. Yes, we have seen Black Lives Matter. Yes, we have seen Bernie Sanders' presidential campaign. But whatever happened to the overall Progressive Movement? It has lost its steely-eyed focus on meaningful reforms, and it no longer offers the hope for progress that it once did.

Unfortunately, more and more of us are giving up. According to 2014 Gallup poll assessing the confidence level citizens have in the three branches of government, the U.S. Congress as a whole registered 7 percent effectiveness—dead last among the three branches. In other words, the vast majority of Americans don't trust their elected representatives to accomplish much during their time in the Washington.

I can single out the Veterans Administration (VA) as an example of the disease afflicting Congress, because I served on the House Committee for Veterans' Affairs for twenty years, and I spent four years as its chairman.

For years, the VA had been under pressure to provide better services to its clients. When I became chairman of the committee in 2007, I regularly scheduled hearings to deal with recurring issues within the VA bureaucracy. One of the more pressing issues during my tenure was the rising suicide rate among vets.

An example of VA incompetence came about when the agency decided to help veterans quit smoking. They prescribed the smoking cessation drug Chantix. Despite credible warnings from the FDA that Chantix could cause suicidal thoughts, VA doctors continued to treat patients diagnosed with PTSD—a mental condition whose victims don't need any encouragement to harm themselves—with Chantix.

The issue came to national prominence when the psychiatric ward of the Dallas VA had to shut down in early 2008 after four patients committed suicide. When VA administrators figured out that Chantix was linked to the deaths, they suggested to doctors that they could continue to treat patients with the suicide-inducing drug—but suggested they change the patients' diagnoses from PTSD to "adjustment disorder."

In my opening remarks before the full Committee on the day of the hearing investigating this real crime, I said, "Same old pattern ... deny, deny, deny. When caught, cover up, cover up, cover up. No one is held accountable, and the system goes on. When are things going to change? When is someone going to be held accountable? When will they understand it's not about the process, but about the veteran?"

My years on the House Committee for Veterans' Affairs taught me that those of us who wanted better treatment for our vets were knocking our head against a solid wall called "process," which bureaucrats used with great effectiveness to ward off changes that were not in their best interests. They also faced refusal not only to increase funding for any branch of government, but even a refusal to transfer existing resources to help those in need. A new aircraft carrier or bomber was much more important to the government than helping our wounded veterans.

During my years in Congress, I observed that legislative leaders used this same idea of "process" to stifle change, to protect their fiefdoms, their power, and their position, and to ensure their reelection. These rules, traditions, and procedures are used as roadblocks to anyone trying to accomplish anything significant.

How "process" can thwart change may not be obvious to some. The whole "process" equation leaves out the human element. If someone dies as the result of a policy, then it's the failure of the "protocols" that were used. How can anyone be held accountable for that? It never takes into account that the vet who hanged himself using his own T-shirt in a VA psychiatric ward was struggling with his smoking habit and also suffering from PTSD—and should have been informed of the possible side effects of the drugs he was taking.

In my mind, these vets were not victims of a "process"—or a "misdiagnosis," as VA administrators said, trying to cover up their ineptitude. They were casualties of a war they weren't even aware they were fighting: the war against change, the ongoing battle to beat back any attempt to run the government in an efficient manner.

So what do our elected officials give us? Instead of solutions, we have studies. Instead of holding people accountable, we accept "a failure of procedure." Nothing changes. The ball rolls on. As a Democrat, it would be easy for me to blame the Republicans for the lack of progress on critical issues, but that wouldn't be true. The problem is that *no one* in Congress possesses the leadership skills necessary to bridge the divide and bring people together. The problem stems from the Democratic Party leadership's failure to clearly articulate what we stand for.

The recent VA scandal concerning falsified appointment logs is a perfect example of this. Not one Democrat took a stand. Instead, the two parties came up with a deal that didn't solve anything.

I want to make clear that I have always been pro-veteran and anti-war. These are two separate issues: the first is human, and the second is political. Political decisions drive us to war. It's our citizens who come home with the wounds of war. That's why I fought hard to keep us out of wars we had no business fighting. Capricious military adventures are never in our best national interest. We can fearlessly take that stand as Democrats while still maintaining our patriotic fervor.

Caring for our veterans is part of the cost of war. Unfortunately, we have not fulfilled our commitment to the brave soldiers who return home. Democrats must take the lead in caring for veterans' physical and mental well-being, because the toll on the lives of military personnel—physically, emotionally, and spiritually—is incalculable. The human cost of war will never show up in line items in a national budget. That real price is written in the flesh and blood of our soldiers and their families, who every day of their lives bear the scars of battle long after the war has become only a national memory.

I would never seek to compromise the security of our nation over a rigid ideological stance. But I believe it is in the best interests of our soldiers and citizens to take an anti-war stance when it's appropriate.

When I explain my position that entering into war must be carefully and thoughtfully considered because of the human cost, people understand what I'm talking about, especially when I'm speaking to veterans' groups across the nation, which I did often when I was a congressman. Almost everyone in those crowds had first-hand knowledge of what it means to go into combat. They appreciate that I have their health and welfare at heart. Most men and women I meet don't want our country to cavalierly go into battle. They want to know their lives are valued.

I am perplexed by my party's failure to articulate clear goals and respond appropriately to today's most critical issues. A top leader of the Democratic Party actually told me I shouldn't be so "fanatic" on veterans issues, because "they'll never vote for us!" Effective leaders are able to explain their positions on critical issues in ways that people will truly understand. Then they take action. These leadership traits are missing within the Democratic Party as it stands today.

In the past, progressive legislators were effective because they never forgot how they arrived at the halls of power to begin with: their ability to organize around the needs of their constituents—the people they served. As we have already observed, when politicians are more concerned with the "process" of how the law works and not the *people* the laws are designed to serve, the opportunity to seek meaningful change is lost. Momentum shifts from what works for the people to what works for those in power.

Before we go too much further, I want to help clarify what the Progressive Movement has traditionally stood for. This will serve as the basis for much of our discussion.

What Is a Progressive?

The Progressive Era began in the late nineteenth century as a worker reaction to the abuses of the wealthy. There was a time in America when children as young as ten worked in factories for twelve to eighteen hours a day, six days a week. Women were considered too fragile to be given the responsibility of voting. When a worker in a factory lost an arm or a hand or a foot to an industrial accident, he would be sent home without any compensation or medical treatment.

During this time, the Sherman Anti-Trust Act was passed, effectively ending many of the monopolistic practices of some of the largest corporations. The referendum and recall laws were passed to break up machine politics and weed out political corruption.[2] With the New Deal, many of these reforms were solidified. Collective bargaining was no longer considered a "communist conspiracy." Social Security provided a basic safety net for retirees. These were a few of the many reforms that helped lift workers out of poverty and into the middle class. Attempts were also made to reform voting and Jim Crow discrimination laws, but little progress was made on those issues before the 1960s.

By the early sixties, when I arrived on the Cornell University campus, the Progressive Movement had changed its focus. The Civil Rights Movement, under the leadership of Dr. King and others, began to gain traction. The Jim Crow

---

2. With today's income inequality, even worse than in the Gilded Age, why hasn't there been a more general opposition? See Steve Fraser, *The Age of Acquiescence: The Life and Death of American Resistance to Organized Wealth and Power* (Boston, MA: Little, Brown & Company, 2015).

laws had disenfranchised African Americans for seventy-plus years. They couldn't register to vote. They couldn't eat in the same restaurants as whites. They were shut out of educational and economic opportunities.

As a Freedom Rider in the summer before my junior year, I saw how effective non-violent action can be to move the levers of government to force meaningful change. I learned on the job, so to speak, about how progressive politics worked. I would define a progressive politician as one who is concerned first about the needs of the people. Progressives work for equal access to economic and social benefits for all citizens.

The Kennedy and Johnson years ushered in the Great Society programs that included Medicare—which extended healthcare to millions—as well as anti-poverty initiatives, educational reforms, and housing and urban development programs. As great as those reforms were, it was the local organizing by civil rights activists in the Deep South that forced the issue of social reform. It was their willingness to march, to demonstrate, to go to jail, and to risk their lives that drove a Democratic president and Congress to finally hear the issues and respond.

Progressives are first and foremost organizers. They work in their communities, marshaling the genuine aspirations of the citizens for a better life, safe neighborhoods, better schools, and access to healthcare. There is no rugged individualist in the Progressive Movement. There may be idiosyncratic leaders, but they still lead by walking in the shoes of the group they seek to help. I learned that by observing the leaders of the Freedom Rides. I learned that again when I ran for the San Diego School Board.

The Civil Rights Movement, the Environmental Movement, the Women's Movement, the Gay Rights Movement—all of these movements were able to be heard in Congress because of the Democratic Congressional majority that held until 1994.

It's no coincidence that when Kennedy was president and Bobby Kennedy was in the Justice Department, people felt they could be heard. King and others who were fighting for civil rights knew there was someone who would hear them and be sympathetic. The Democratic majority allowed progress to be made—but it doesn't necessarily follow that we can't make progress when we're not in control.

Today, there is a Progressive Caucus in Congress made up of about fifty Democrats. There are progressive think tanks. There are progressive legislators such as Senators Bernie Sanders and Elizabeth Warren, but they seem to have stepped into a vacuum. They just don't know how to get publicity or define themselves as a collective whole. The recent sit-in on the House floor to try to move gun safety legislation forward is an example of what we should be doing all the time!

Why don't they have an effective and unified voice?

The current leadership in Congress is more interested in making sure they remain in power than in putting forward any great ideas. They have lost their way and are not learning from what has worked in the past. They've lost the will to organize at the grass roots, in the neighborhoods and districts where they began.

We should have absorbed the lesson Newt Gingrich taught us in the late 1980s and early '90s when he used his leadership of the minority position to put out a program. He worked for ten years to come to power behind a detailed platform of programs his political party could rally behind. He even gave it a catchy name: A Contract with America. It was a masterful effort that required patience and determination.

Rather than band together and propose a platform to usher them back into power, the Democrats in Congress still think they can "legislate." But the minority party can't do that in the House of Representatives. The House structure makes their success nearly impossible.

What are the primary issues of the day that most Americans readily associate with progressives? Aid for college? Affordable housing? Job placement? What the Democrats *should* do is use their platform to articulate a coherent progressive position on these issues. But because they're preoccupied with other agendas, they're not being heard. During my more than twenty years of service in Congress, it was a weakness I constantly pointed out.

Democrats have always been portrayed as anti-veteran. This simply isn't true. John Kerry is a prime example of a Democrat who bravely served his country. When I was in Congress, I put forward healthcare programs as a way of "Keeping Our Promise" to our veterans. I wrote the Twenty-First Century GI Bill that made college and home buying possible for our returning heroes. We doubled the VA's budget.

In sum, I always put the veterans right up front as a group that needed our help. Taking that stance made me very acceptable to conservatives, many of whom are veterans who thought the Democrats had ignored them. My entire legislative agenda enjoyed bipartisan support, but even the best Democratic leaders did not understand or adopt this agenda.

I'm not trying to massage my ego here. I'm simply pointing out how a progressive can champion an agenda that will make friends and influence people across the aisle. Putting veterans right at the top of my agenda was not only the right thing to do, but also served as a bridge to my conservative colleagues. It allowed me to be anti-war and pro-veteran simultaneously. I won a lot of respect for my stand.

You don't have to look too hard to find a variety of issues to which a similar approach can be applied. Issues like healthcare, transportation, immigration, college aid, and civil rights can be put into a coherent whole with programs to carry them out. That would garner popular support. At the same time, we have to work collaboratively with outside groups to implement our ideas in an organized way.

Regrettably, Congress has devolved into a body of individual entrepreneurs. Everybody says what they want to say, and there is no organized plan to put forward a coherent agenda. When you say "Democratic Party," the assumption is that there is a platform, but there really isn't one—at least, not one that is clearly articulated and understood by all.

Sometimes the best way to bridge a gap of understanding is to have a positive give-and-take session in which each party gives up as much as it gains. Let's go back to healthcare, an issue to which most Americans can easily relate. The most progressive idea on healthcare today is called "single-payer."

Insurance companies would be phased out and the government would take over paying the healthcare providers. There would still be private doctors, but essentially a single-payer system would be "Medicare for all." Everyone would be eligible.

In entering into these types of negotiations, we have to keep in mind that we already have Medicare. Seniors are able to go to the doctor and the government pays the bill. Senior citizens only have to pay certain premiums. It's an idea that is well understood (despite the pleas of the Tea Party to "keep your government out of our Medicare") and widely accepted.

In the original version of President Obama's program, the Affordable Care Act (ACA), a scaled-down version of a single-payer system called a "public option" played an essential role. The President could not support the single-payer system, because that would mean a proposal for "socialized medicine" coming from our first black chief executive. He did not want to take on the universally hated private insurance companies. When it came to negotiating legislation, Obama decided *before negotiations even began* that he didn't even want the pubic option on the table. It would have caused too much of a ruckus with insurance companies and their lobbyists.

His primary concern was to preserve the private insurance companies—the same companies that most progressives think are the major cause of rising healthcare costs today.

President Obama didn't even make a show of fighting to incorporate progressive values and principles into the healthcare legislation. He let it all slide. If he had made a well-articulated stand up front, I believe that his administration would have been able to pass a more robust, patient-friendly program that could have benefited even more citizens.

Communication is part of the problem. You probably remember hearing a lot of fearful talk about "socialized medicine" from conservatives. The irony is that the platform for an American version of socialized medicine has already been established. People in this country accept Medicare and an even more "socialist" form of government healthcare for veterans. Vets go to government hospitals staffed with government doctors who take care of them because they fought for their country.

We can frame the argument by putting it in different terms. If we use language like "Medicare for all" or "VA care for all," we can't be attacked for introducing socialized medicine. Why? Because people already accept those kinds of medical care. All we're trying to do is broaden those terms to include more people.

On this important issue of greater access to low-cost healthcare, Obama couldn't overcome his greatest weakness as a negotiator. This failure distinguishes him from his Democratic predecessor, Bill Clinton, who labored tirelessly to leverage every legislator's individual interests into the interests of his agenda. While he and Hillary failed on *their* healthcare plan, Clinton was a master at personal rapport building—and still is.

Promoting a Progressive Agenda

It is possible to promote a progressive agenda even when you are a lone voice, if you know how to organize people.

My experience with San Diego politics illustrates a number of ways to champion a progressive agenda. I was one of the few Democrats to consistently win elections in conservative, Republican San Diego. That's because I learned how to put progressive ideas into a context that was acceptable to a wide spectrum of people without giving up my principles. I learned how to talk to the other side.

My first political campaign was for a seat on the Board of the San Diego Unified School District. During my campaign, I talked about each child reaching his or her potential. Naturally, that message appealed to the ambitious parents in the wealthier and whiter northern part of our city, who wanted gifted programs for their talented kids. It also spoke to the poor parents in our southern areas who wanted more resources and increased attention from the Board for their children. So, in the context of each student reaching his or her potential, everyone heard that I supported their kids. The message had wide appeal and didn't pit one group against the other. It was a program everyone could support. As a result, I became the first Democrat in San Diego to defeat an incumbent Republican—for *any* office!

I was re-elected continually; I had a strong base because of my hands-on approach to problem solving. As mayor, I was highly visible. I worked long days, attending every community event you could imagine in my city. I knew the community backward and forward because I was always there. This made it easy for me to find issues that were meaningful to middle-class families. People could *see* me and *touch* me on the issues they truly cared about.

I never found it difficult to discover the hot issues in my community. As a candidate for the School Board, the City Council, and Congress, I went door to door. Every day, my goal was to try to reach one hundred people or more. I would meet them in their homes, on street corners, in stores—wherever—just so I could talk to them about things that really mattered to them.

The former Speaker of the House, Tip O'Neill, used to say that "all politics is local." More clearly stated, every community has a local issue that can provide an observant politician with an opportunity to become the people's advocate. Thanks to my service to the city over the last twenty-five years, there are people who still remember my impact on the community. In their minds, I'm the one who got them their stop signs and new playgrounds. I'm the one who got their kids safely to school where they could now enjoy their sports and games on grass fields. Because I addressed something that really mattered to them, my particular position on something like the war in Iraq—potentially a very divisive issue—didn't really matter. They were in my corner because I had championed a cause that changed the very streets on which they lived.

This is the essence of leadership: gaining the confidence of the people by working on *their* issues. They will then follow *you* on the other issues.

San Diego is a city that is very pro-war, but I was anti-war. Yet, even though I was a peacenik, I won ten elections to Congress and one as mayor. This was not necessarily because they cared less about what was going on with the Iraq War than what was going on in their own communities. What mattered most to them was that I was their champion and advocate. I was their leader. They knew I genuinely cared about them and their interests because I took the time to learn about their neighborhoods and schools. I learned their languages, foods, and customs. I even went to a Filipino dance studio to learn Filipino dances.

Our leaders need to be physically seen at Little League games, school graduations, PTA meetings, and homeless encampments. I was everywhere. Just recently, as I was walking through Skid Row in Los Angeles, two very weary homeless men called out: "Aren't you the guy in San Diego who's trying to help us?" How very gratifying!

I can't stress enough the number of loyal followers (and voters) we will gain by offering that personal touch. When you can show people you care about the issues that affect their quality of life, they will listen to you and trust you on everything else. The issues that concern people in their neighborhoods don't fall easily along party lines. When you help people, they couldn't care less whether you are a Democrat or a Republican. They just want their problem solved.

Crime is another example of how progressive politicians can gain support for our overall agenda. Traditionally, Democrats and progressives have been seen as soft on crime because many of the people they are serving, especially minorities, see themselves correctly as victims of the police. We know that poverty and poor education lead to crime. My approach in San Diego was simple: instead of just talking about the community's perception of policing and the politics that surround it, I decided to do something about it.

In my district, where most of the people are poor and black or Hispanic, we made policing more effective by expanding what is called "community policing." The police became embedded in the community. There are a hundred ways to do that—it can begin by police walking the sidewalks rather than riding in their patrol cars. They visit schools. They visit stores. They are generally "around" and highly visible in the community, not just when a crisis occurs. They are inviting and approachable. People have their cellphone numbers. Kids talk to them and they talk to kids. In this setting, the police see human beings, and the community sees the officers as a human beings.

It turns out that if you do that in a rigorous way, the community trusts the police. It fosters an entirely new sense that the police are actually *protecting* the community, not oppressing it.

The cops always endorsed me in elections. Their labor setting was a factor—they were also part of a collective bargaining unit. But they also knew that I was enthusiastic about them because my district trusted them. Here I was, a progressive going after crime and giving money to cops in a way that everybody loved. The conservatives loved it. The cops loved it. I was probably the only urban city council member in the United States who could walk into an all-black and Hispanic audience with the chief of police and neighborhood cops by my side and get a standing ovation!

This is another example of how a progressive can take issues and put them into a different context, coming up with something that everyone can support. If you follow this plan, you will not be considered some isolated, wild-eyed radical. Instead, you will be viewed as a genuine implementer of positive change that affects the entire community.

The Problem with Progressives

Of course, progressives have a tough job. By definition, we must step on the toes of some entrenched interests. Given the power of the healthcare industry, it's hard to pass health reform. Given the power of the banks, it's hard to pass financial reform. And the list goes on and on.

Why, then, should *we* be bought off by those interests? Unfortunately, when progressive candidates rely on these same people for their money, they often fail to remember that nothing's free.

So what's the answer? Get private money out of politics. Educate the people on the need for small donations.

Senator Bernie Sanders showed this vividly. If every supporter gave ten dollars, a candidate would have enough money to run a campaign. Of course, in today's politically charged environment, no politician thinks this would be enough. Instead, politicians rely on $25,000 and $100,000 contributions. Suddenly, the politician is beholden to the donors, and our progressivism is lost—or at least severely compromised.

That is, in sum, my answer to the question, "Whatever happened to the Progressive Movement?" The answer is, we have lost our sense of identity because we have failed to clearly articulate our positions. And we've lost our sense of community-based, grassroots strategy because big money allows us to move away from the power of organizing, which put us in power to begin with.

As powerless as this may make us feel, I don't believe we can give up hope. We can regain both our confidence and our efficacy if we make an overall commitment to the people. We must recommit ourselves to making it our top priority to champion the simplest of issues that affect everyday citizens. This is how we can gain widespread support, even when our party is in the minority.

Progressives can—and will—regain forward momentum when we commit ourselves to forging relationships that eventually reach across political lines. We must rise to the challenge by thinking outside the box in how we approach and frame critical issues that reflect the values and principles of our party.

This is progressive politics. These are progressive values. It is our job to reclaim, reinforce, and reemploy them for the good of the entire nation.

FOUR

Some Key Progressive Ideas

There are those who look at things the way they are, and ask why? I dream of things that never were, and ask why not?
—Robert F. Kennedy

After the mid-term elections of 2010, the Democrats lost their majority position in the House and the power shifted to the Republicans. Progressive leadership before the elections was in disarray. Progressives had lost their sense of identity as reformers, and they sorely lacked the organizational ability to confront the many issues facing our nation.[3]

---

3. But see the role of the Koch Brothers' stealth efforts in Chapter 10, "The Shellacking: Dark Money's Midterm Debut, 2010" in Jane Mayer, *Dark Money: The Hidden History of the Billionaires Behind the Rise of the Radical Right* (New York: Doubleday, 2016).

But now that they are in the minority position, their ability to effect change can be even more formidable. The structure of the House doesn't allow the minority party to legislate effectively, but that doesn't mean they can't be effective voices for change. I think back to what Newt Gingrich accomplished in the early '90s, when the Republicans had been out of power in the House of Representatives for decades. He set an agenda and made his party stick to it. He promised change when they came to power. That's what Progressive politicians need to do: set the agenda that will have the most meaningful effects once we get back into power. There are a number of real opportunities for gaining traction and effecting change.

One of the most pressing issues facing Progressives today is how to overcome the gerrymandering that has fixed districts according to party affiliation. This strategy is often used to unfairly establish a majority for either party as incumbents use the redistricting process to guarantee themselves lifetime seats in office. Elected officials pick their constituents—not the other way around.

Incumbents, of course, have a built-in advantage, and there are few districts in the country where elections can take place on a level playing field. More often than not, competition is eliminated or minimized by the use of gerrymandering, whereby the same individuals are constantly reelected and the same party always dominates. This limited competition inevitably limits turnover in Congress.

To make matters worse, once one party becomes the majority, there's very little incentive for them to talk to the other side. This is why we have gridlock in Congress today.

Everyone appeals only to their own base, and they are more worried about the next election than the general good. Rather than engaging in real negotiations over how best to resolve major issues of governance, they take a safe approach and only vote for the interests of their own base. This situation is by nature truly anti-democratic—it stops all conversation and debate.

There needs to be a national movement that calls for policies that are both stricter and more fair regarding drawing district lines for local, state, and national offices. This has been effective in Arizona and California. More and more states are authorizing Independent Redistricting Commissions. Such a law was adopted in Arizona through Proposition 11, unanimously approved by the electorate. Redistricting was removed from the state legislators and given to an Independent Commission.

Proposition 11 so upset the incumbent politicians that they sued to overturn the law. They argued that, since the new rule was adopted through the proposition process and not by elected legislators, it violated the "Elections Clause" of the U.S. Constitution. Thankfully, the Supreme Court of the United States saw through that fallacious argument, stating that "the electorate shares lawmaking authority on equal footing with the Arizona Legislature. The voters may adopt laws and constitutional amendments by ballot initiative, and they may approve or disapprove, by referendum, measures passed by the Legislature."

All states should adopt "Independent Commissions" that are not tied directly to one party and would have the power to draw districts without the influence of the State Legislature. The Commission itself could be selected in a number of ways, but the priority is that such commissions would be independent of party designations. The number of truly contested districts would skyrocket—and democratic debate and increased participation by voters would follow.

We see this positive direction in California, which established an independent redistricting commission after the 2010 census. So far, the changes have resulted in some of the most competitive state and federal congressional races in the nation.

For a number of years when I was in Congress, I fought against gerrymandering. To my surprise, my harshest critics were not Republicans—it was my own party that frequently viewed me as a pariah. The people who were supposed to stand beside me and "have my back" had themselves become self-absorbed and invested in maintaining the status quo. So it's not just the Republicans who benefit from gerrymandering. It is all incumbents.

The Tea Party—and the Trumpeteers

I personally am attracted to voices within our party that are passionately calling for change in our culture; there aren't enough of those voices. Over time, I have developed a different view of the existing political scene that I don't think is shared by many other Democrats or Progressives. Specifically, I'm talking about the Tea Party—and its logical evolution into the Trump phenomenon.

Our political situation is so dire that I've spent a great deal of time studying what is working so effectively for the

Some Key Progressive Ideas

Republican Party. I've scrutinized their agendas and strategies, even attending Tea Party and Trump rallies and membership meetings so I could see, up close, what is going on and who is involved.

I was quite surprised—they were not who I expected. Although there were a fair number of white supremacists and religious zealots, I saw a lot of regular folks—the kind of people who don't have the best job prospects, who maybe don't even have healthcare, and who are concerned about how they're going to pay for their kids' college educations. Frankly, they looked a lot like the rest of the lower-to-middle class—people who are swiftly being squeezed out of a more prosperous future.

Many of them were white—in fact, people of color were noticeably absent. While they were passionately calling for change and talking about the same kinds of issues discussed at any progressive rally, there was hardly anyone of color in attendance.

I bring up the issue of race because it is a significant one. Many of the people at these rallies expressed concern that if America stays on its current path, their children will be worse off than they currently are. Seeing and hearing this got me thinking: *Shouldn't these people join with us? Progressives have the exact same concerns!*

Republicans, however, have already beaten us to the punch with a blatantly racist appeal. They've done a terrifyingly effective job of convincing these people that the Republican Party is the best party for them because they stand for the middle-class, white values of decades past.

People at these rallies seem to want an America that is all but disappearing—one-income households, a homogenous social and political life where everyone looks and thinks like them, and a rugged individualism where everyone takes care of their own family's needs, despite the complexities of modern life. Republicans use race to divide Americans by claiming they are not getting the economic and social deal they were promised as the middle-class. That message got people's attention.

Many of these people are literally struggling to survive, and the GOP has cleverly used this to their advantage. They've convinced them that none of the other issues are more important than race. Race, then—the shared experience of the white middle-class promise—becomes the basis of their common bond.

No wonder the Tea Party and Trumpeteers hate Obama. Sure, the Republican establishment may have turned them against Democrats in general, but Obama's race was always a fundamental issue, whether or not it was openly discussed.

Sadly, the exploitation of race as a wedge issue is nothing new. Historically, this has often been the case in American society. Drawing attention to race has long been a political tactic for keeping people from joining together for a common cause. Whites say, "I ain't gonna unite with the blacks," or blacks won't unite with Hispanics or Asians. Wherever the line in the sand is drawn, it perpetuates itself. It's a vicious cycle.

We can, however, overcome this divide by uniting over *real* issues. For instance, the governor of North Carolina recently refused to expand Medicare in his state, which forced a district hospital and its emergency room in rural Bellhaven to close.

Having no emergency services within a hundred miles of the city would have resulted in many unnecessary deaths.

So, in an uncharacteristic but admirable move, the white Mayor—a conservative Republican—joined forces with local black pastors and the NAACP. Together, they worked against North Carolina's governor and Congress in an effort to restore their hospital. They not only organized a 300-mile walk to Washington, but they also filed a Civil Rights complaint. And they won.

When it comes to life-and-death issues that concern everyone—Republicans and Democrats, conservatives and liberals—there's plenty of room to unite and work together. We just have to be willing to sit down with some of the Tea Party and Trumpeteers and find out what they're really interested in. Issues like education, healthcare, and jobs have always been topics for generating dialogue across party lines.

We can take it a step further by conducting focus groups to poll the Republican constituency, determining their primary issues and concerns. We must assess which issues are of greatest interest to them so that we can devise a strategy to address these issues.

Finding common ground always propels change and affects lives. Whenever you can get people to work together on a common goal—whether it's education, healthcare, or jobs—the race issue becomes less important. People begin to look at one another less and instead focus on the outcome. They stop saying, "He doesn't look like me," and start asking, "What does this mean for our kids? How will it directly benefit us and our community?"

I've seen this time and again in my own political work. Once we get people focused on making education better for our kids or making our community better, race ends up being less important. Finding the right ideas, goals, or programs may take some thought and experimentation in the beginning stages, but identifying common goals is a proven strategy for unification. It can—and should—be done.

The Tobin Tax

Tax relief, in my opinion, is a key issue where we could beat conservatives at their own game. Republicans are strongly opposed to raising taxes, as we all know. But there are a number of creative ways to finance the government other than continually raising taxes and fees. The Tobin Tax—named after its creator, Nobel Laureate James Tobin, the late economist from Yale—is a radical idea for tax relief that I believe would appeal to the Tea Party and Trumpeters. It offers a strategy for bringing income taxes to *zero* while still *increasing* necessary revenues for the federal government.

We owe the Tobin Tax to an idea that originated during the presidency of Richard Nixon. In the early 1970s, Nixon announced that the United States dollar would no longer be convertible to gold. This sent seismic shocks around the globe—the U.S. dollar was fast becoming the sole backing of other currencies, and Nixon's announcement had the potential to wreak massive havoc on the international economy.

Enter James Tobin, a well-respected American macroeconomist who had been awarded the Nobel Prize for economics. Tobin proposed a new system for international currency stability, one that would include an international charge on foreign-exchange transactions. This would cushion exchange-rate fluctuations.

The Tobin Tax is predicated on a very simple idea: on any transaction involving exchange rate movements (or any other financial "bet" not based on real assets), a small tax would be levied—e.g., 0.25 percent of the volume of the transaction. The tax would be small enough that bets would still be made, but because of the trillions of dollars of transactions involved *per day*, the income would be enormous.

Most of these transactions or bets on currency rates and other derivative areas are international in scope and would require international enforcement for full effect. Tobin taxes have substantial potential to prevent financial crises. The estimated hundreds of billions they would generate each year for the U.S. alone would make it possible to address urgent national and global priorities such as poverty, hunger, and global warming.

Here's a breakdown of how Tobin-style taxes might work:

- Currency speculators trade over three trillion dollars each day across borders. The market is huge and volatile.

- Each trade would be taxed at 0.1 to 0.25 percent of volume (about 10 to 25 cents per hundred dollars).

- Taxes would focus on short-term speculative trades but leave long-term productive investments intact.

- The currency market would thus shrink in volume, helping to restore national economic autonomy. Nations could once again intervene effectively to protect their own currency from devaluation and financial crisis.

- Billions in revenue would be generated for any nation that imposed such a tax.

- Revenue could actually replace the income tax!

To get the attention of our Tea Party and Trump friends and to draw more individuals to the Progressive Movement, we must appeal to the everyday concerns of their constituents. Something as radical and yet commonsense as the Tobin Tax could be a way of accomplishing this goal.

The overall objective, of course, is to get groups to look at issues in an entirely new way. The Democratic Party has always been viewed as the high-tax party. Introducing an idea as unorthodox as the Tobin plan provides clear evidence of our party's ability and willingness to find ways to increase revenue *without* increasing domestic taxes, especially on the middle class. That's the kind of message to which even a staunch Republican might be willing to listen.

There definitely are tactical and logistical considerations for implementing something as large in scale as the Tobin Tax, as it would require cooperation from other countries. There would have to be a solid international agreement, and certain countries would be more apt to jump onboard than others. But even if the tax never actually went through, Progressives would be seen as exercising real leadership. An initiative like the Tobin Tax could potentially demonstrate how a revolutionary goal can unite people. It would catalyze a new kind of movement, one that would involve the Tea Party, Trumpeteers, *and* progressive Democrats, working side by side.

The Road to Revolutionary Ideas

Free college is another example of a revolutionary idea that has the potential to unite people across party lines. Merely saying "free college" sparks debate over how we're going to pay for it. At the same time, given the rising cost of a college education, we've automatically drawn the interest of a large segment of the American population who are struggling to afford the cost of college.

We may not, at this very moment, have the perfect solution for how to fund a free college education for all Americans. However, by using this kind of language—as Bernie Sanders has shown—our voice and message will resonate with the majority of Americans. This is an issue that has tremendous relevance and emotional power for them.

The ultimate question is, how do you get people who are on the other side (at least on a superficial level) to work with you?

The answer is to give them a revolutionary idea they can get behind. The road to revolution is paved with good ideas.

We need to make our nation more democratic and open up the election process to more varied voices by creating independent commissions to draw political districts. By doing this, we can invigorate the electorate and bring change to our legislative bodies. It would even reduce corruption and the power of special interests, which are endemic in all state capitals and in Washington.

What binds most Americans together is a belief we can build a better life, one more satisfying than our parents had. We are a can-do people. What we need is grassroots leadership that will invigorate the national conversation about the direction of our nation.

We need some dramatic new ideas that blunt the racial wedge and unite people instead of dividing them. A few of the many pressing concerns that could become part of the Progressive agenda include:

- The Tobin Tax
- A commitment to solve the homelessness issue with a national housing campaign
- Free college for everyone who wants it
- Better Yale than jail—real solutions for incarcerated youth
- Safe neighborhoods

Bold, revolutionary ideas are needed to win back public support. The Democratic Party needs to craft a new vocabulary that reaches *all* of our neighbors. Our Progressive values of education, healthcare, and job creation have remained constant. We just need to regain our sense of clarity and hone our ability to convey these values and principles in a way that gains support—not just from politicians, but from the everyday citizens who will benefit by the choices we make.

FIVE

Acting Locally: What Does Your Community Need?

All politics is local.
—Tip O'Neill

Organizing as a Way of Understanding

Modern American political life runs on the notion that power can best be maintained by manipulating the political structure. One example of that comes dramatically into play if you're a congressman. Every two years we are elected from the districts we represent. After each census, state legislators undertake to jigger the borders of the districts they represent or the ones they expect to run in, in order to tilt the odds in their favor.

This is gerrymandering, and it has become a way of maintaining a power base for both parties. Gerrymandering has served to make the political process less competitive by keeping new voices out of power. This is one reason I have been so adamant about the need to vest all districting authority in independent commissions.

District 50, which I represented for nearly ten years, was gerrymandered after the 2000 census. Juan Vargas, a rival for many years and then a member of the California State Assembly, soon to be termed out of his seat, had the borders of District 50 reconfigured to include Imperial County, a rural area with a significant Hispanic population. I had represented that district for ten years, so my base was established within San Diego city borders.

I had developed, through methodical organizing, a precise understanding of the needs of the different neighborhoods within my district. I was a true city boy with a keen sense of the problems facing my constituents. Now, suddenly, part of the district I represented had a very different demographic and economic makeup.

Vargas's intentions were clear—he planned to run for my seat in Congress in the 2004 election, after his term ended. He figured that, since Imperial County was primarily agricultural and had a population that was more than 80 percent Hispanic, I would be vulnerable, because I knew little about agriculture while he would be received with open arms.

I remember looking over a map of Imperial County. This part of my new district, called District 51, had a population of only 160,000. Comprising more than 4,000 square

Acting Locally: What Does Your Community Need?

miles of desert, bordered on the north and west by Riverside and San Diego Counties, and by Mexico and Arizona to the south and east, Imperial County received only three inches of annual rainfall. Amazingly, the district's primary industry was agriculture and beef production, because of its proximity to Colorado River water. Extensive irrigation had transformed the desert sand into productive lettuce and grape ranches.

The only thing I knew about lettuce was where to buy it. I knew nothing about the issues facing farmers and ranchers. I learned that Imperial had one of the highest poverty rates in California, and one of the lowest high school graduation rates—and I knew that poor academic success usually perpetuates the cycle of poverty.

Imperial Country was a large area with a small population, one I could ignore and still win reelection because it represented a small portion of the total population of my district. But because of my passion for community organizing, every community means something to me. I knew that this rather isolated and small portion of my district was made up of people with real needs.

Despite all the questions that flooded my mind about this unfamiliar area of California, it wasn't in my nature to be intimidated by a challenge. I knew what lay behind the strategy of changing the borders of my district. The traditional way of political thinking didn't surprise me at all. The political machine that functioned on its mastery of the "process of government" would only work in Imperial County if I let it. I knew that practicing the art of organizing at the level of people's concerns could counteract the machine, if I put the effort into it.

I had a surprise for Mr. Vargas.

As soon as I saw the new borders of District 51, I knew exactly what had to be done. I didn't yet understand the primary issues that concerned my constituents, but I knew how to learn. I knew from my campaign experiences that, if I approached people with a willingness to listen, I could learn what was on their minds. I knew that if I set aside any preconceived notions of what their needs were, they would open up to me.

I set out on a fact-finding mission that was also a journey of discovery. I needed to learn about the culture of Imperial County. It's naïve to think that culture doesn't matter anymore and that we are all just one big happy melting pot of ethnicities and values—as of everyone listens to the same music, eats the same foods, and has the same aspirations. That's what media-driven campaigning techniques require us to believe, but that's not reality.

And there was another reality I had to overcome. I was a liberal, Jewish congressman heading full steam into a very conservative community dominated by growers and ranchers who probably hadn't voted for a Democrat in their lifetimes. The county included an impoverished electorate who resided in the bottom echelons of the socio-economic makeup of the area. I felt certain they had never seen a United States Congressman attend any of their functions.

Acting Locally: What Does Your Community Need?

Organizing by Drinking a Soda

The day I drove into El Centro, the Imperial County seat, had to be the hottest day of the year. Only later did someone tell me summer was just warming up, and summers there often reach 120 degrees.

But the biggest challenge for me wasn't the heat—it was the fact that not a soul in town even knew my name. I had set up some appointments with county officials to introduce myself, and I had a little time on my hands before those meetings, so I stopped in a local café for a soda.

In a far corner of the café, I saw a group of old-timers sitting around shooting the breeze. I asked if I could join them. I introduced myself as their new congressman, and quite frankly, none of them seemed too shocked to meet me. After we were done chatting, one of them said to me, "After this you're going over to the county building to meet with some of the county officials." They knew my schedule. I was impressed and taken aback. "How did you know my schedule?"

"We know everything," this guy said to me. "We just sit here."

That conversation gave me pause. They obviously knew who to talk to, because it didn't take long for my name to get around the area. I think it took about five minutes before the grapevine in El Centro began to buzz.

There are only three population centers in Imperial County—Calexico, El Centro, and Brawley. Each town had a similar café where the regulars met. All the small-town dynamics you would see in any Smalltown, USA operated in these population centers. Even in larger communities, these gathering places exist.

I didn't have to drive a hundred miles to sip a soda. I could have run TV ads and sent mailers using a list furnished by the Democratic Congressional Campaign Committee. I could have scheduled radio interviews and sent letters of introductions to newspaper editors, local government officials, and people like that. But that's not organizing, in my book.

Eventually, I would need to do those things during a campaign. But initially, I wanted to meet the people where they lived—the farmers, the ranchers, the farm workers, the union organizers, and students, teachers, and business people. I knew I could get so much more done by talking face to face. Yes, this method requires more time and attention than any other way of meeting constituents, but it's the only way to truly understand the people, their culture, and their situations.

Since I was a liberal Democrat with a decidedly progressive bent, most people expected me to simply ignore the farmers and ranchers. What did a city boy from New York know about farming? And the growers were die-hard Republicans. They would never vote for Bob Filner.

But that's not my way of thinking. I always believe I can bridge differences by listening to people's needs. Farmers are small businessmen and women; they are fathers and community leaders. They had to have some issues on which we could develop mutual ground. I believe that political labels give us only a superficial understanding of each other.

When I showed up offering to hear them out on anything that might be on their minds, why wouldn't they talk to me? I'm not naïve enough to believe I can please everyone, nor do I even need to try. But it's just not in me to ignore people.

I hit all the key places in each of the three major communities. I visited high schools, social service agencies, and labor unions. I spoke with church leaders and met with the editors of local newspapers. I sought out city planners to discuss the issues they faced in building infrastructure and public works. I looked for issues that had a federal bent, ones I could help them with—and ones that were winnable.

Up and down the dry hills and across the scorched roads of Imperial County, I met farmers in their fields and ranchers on their ranches. My goal was never to tackle the big issues right away. I wouldn't walk up to a farmer and ask him or her where they stand on the Iraq war or try to discuss the national budget. None of that would help them deal with the issues they face.

My immediate goal was to find an issue that was small enough to win, but important enough to their lives to matter. Because I focused on smaller issues first, they began to get to know me as a problem-solver. My party affiliation, my political philosophy, and how I voted on the Iraq war became secondary issues—if we ever got around to talking about them at all.

My habit was to show up at the farmer's front door and simply ask him, "Can you tell me how you farm?" It may sound ignorant, but you would be surprised how they responded to me. They were more than willing to talk about their operations. Many of them seemed pleased to have me even ask.

One day, under a hot morning sun, I listened to a farmer in his lettuce field. This man, whom I had just met, patiently and graciously walked me through the economics of growing lettuce. He plucked a fresh head of lettuce off a plant and held it up to me. "See this head of romaine? I can sell this for a dime. But if I strip off the outside leaves, I can sell the romaine leaves for twenty to forty cents each. If I take everything off but the heart, I can package what's left as heart of romaine, and I can get a buck for it. Then if I shred it up and add some croutons and sell it as a Caesar salad, I can get three dollars. That's how I do farming."

He didn't have any big problems he wanted me to solve that day. He just wanted to talk about his operation. I didn't have any way to help him, so I just listened. He became a supporter, and I acquired a lasting understanding of the economics of lettuce growing.

Every community has a power structure; Imperial County is no different. Voting is usually sharply divided and predictable. In Imperial Valley, the people voted Democratic—but the money, the power, and the influence lay with the big growers and ranchers, and with the newspaper editors. These were the guys who did the major hiring in the county, and they were staunchly Republican.

Yet the people of Imperial County constantly were surprised that I took the time to speak to them and to listen to their concerns. One even said to me in a group meeting, with real surprise in his voice, "Wow, this Democratic liberal commie is out here talking to us." But why not? I represented them! The conventional wisdom said that the growers weren't going to support me—but I never accepted the conventional wisdom. Instead, I looked for problems I could help them with. This worked to break down the ideological barriers that party labels are designed to create.

One particular issue that struck close to home for these farmers was the inheritance tax. In my meetings with them, they constantly brought up how their wealth rested in their land—land they had worked hard to develop, using their own resources to turn desert into arable and productive acreage. These farmers weren't huge, multi-national corporations; most of them had been raised in farming families. This was their way of life. But because of the inheritance tax—the so-called "death tax"—their kids would not be able to enjoy the fruits of their labor. The inheritance tax stood at 50 percent. After the death of the family patriarch or matriarch, the farm almost always would have to be sold to pay that tax.

This tax struck at the very heart of the traditional family farm. When the estate tax legislation came up in the House, I voted against my ideology—but for my farmers. This was something I could get behind, not only because it was good for my constituents, but also because—in the case of the family farmer—it was penalizing the wrong group of people.

These guys were not corporate farmers bent on cornering a market through inter-generational wealth. They were hard-working, small-business people who sincerely cared about their industry and about the production of food. Their children were deeply involved in their operations, so why shouldn't the next generation be able to benefit from a lifetime of work?

I voted so often to help the family farmer that one Imperial Valley newspaper editor wrote about how I was voting with my constituents. The article had a real effect across the Imperial Valley. People knew I would listen to their concerns and work to do something for them.

Listening is always invaluable. I found most of my constituents to be very interesting people; they were talented businessmen who had a lot to say about their profession, and often they were accomplished in other areas as well. Simply showing up has a salutary effect on people. One thing I can bring to a community as an outsider is a unique perspective.

Visits that promote discussions will help to break down barriers and encourage those who feel powerless to speak up. That very thing happened on several occasions, but one day at a high school in Brawley stands out. I had been invited to speak to a class, and quite frankly, it wasn't going too well. The kids were pretty quiet, even though I was doing my best to get them to open up. We had been discussing wages and jobs, so I asked a fairly simple question: "Don't you think you need more money per hour to live around here?" I was referring to the minimum wage.

A white kid in the back of the room spoke up right away. "I earn enough. I don't need no increase in the minimum wage. What is this bullshit?"

A little Mexican-American girl sitting in the front row turned on him and said, "Yeah, but your father owns the farm." This was a brash statement from a girl who, I later found out, hardly ever spoke up in class.

Boy, did that light the fuse on a stick of dynamite that had been waiting to explode. The class fell into a heated discussion, back and forth, about the work in the fields, how hard it was, and how underpaid some of their parents were.

Afterward, the principal and teacher accused me of trying to polarize the school. I told them, right to their faces, that the school was already polarized. The discontent had been simmering under the surface. That was why they needed to talk about those issues, before they blew up in their faces.

If the topic hadn't blown up when it did, the kids would have carried around a deep feeling of oppression and hurt that would have expressed itself somewhere, somehow. Maybe that's one of the reasons the high school graduation rates were so low in the county. A significant portion of the kids just gave up hope that their lives could be any better.

"You have to talk about this," I told the school officials. "If you can get the kids to see one another's points of view, it will broaden their understanding of the world they live in." I hoped it also might motivate them to seek change, and that is the great fear teachers and principals have.

There was no doubt in my mind that a lot of the kids carried around with them a deep sense of hopelessness. They were hemmed in on all sides in their tiny valley—economically, racially, and geographically—with limited opportunities. In the course of my many discussions with high school students across the valley, it didn't take me long to figure out that most of them had very limited career aspirations. The best-paying jobs in the county were positions as border patrol agents and prison guards at the local federal and state institutions. That was the best hope for a better life for many of them. These were jobs that would take them away from low-paid agricultural work, but never beyond the boundaries of the familiar.

These kinds of entrenched, intergenerational socio-economic problems can't be solved by one U.S. Congressman. But I knew I could do something. My plan was to open as many doors as I could, for as many as I could, while I had the power to do it.

Organizing Empowers the Powerless

Saul Alinsky, the great organizer of the early twentieth century, observed that, "the present power age defines and evaluates everything in terms of power."[4] Those who have economic and social power run the show and call the shots.

We tend to think of power as only existing on a civic, corporate, or national level, but that is wrong. Power operates in every home, every school, and every community, be it a village or a town or a major city. I like to think of power in terms of the ability to make the best choices for our lives. I don't believe people choose impoverishment as much as they think; it chooses them. They have few, if any, other options—because they have no power.

If people feel powerless to change their lives, this feeling alone is often enough to defeat them. So the goal of effective organizing is to empower people, giving them the sense that their lives, and the choices that make up their lives, are in their own hands—at least to the extent they are willing to

---

4. Saul D. Alinsky, *Reveille for Radicals* (New York: Vintage Books, 1989), 53.

put forth the effort to make the best use of the opportunities before them. Parents, teachers, mentors, community leaders, and church leaders all operate on a personal level. They all have the ability, within their circles of influence, to pass along ideas of what is possible.

But what about government? Many think that government only works at a higher level—that those who govern are more concerned about the already powerful and about currying favor with them to stay in office and win elections. But that's not my view of how government works best. As much as I had to work on taxes, or healthcare, or the national budget, with its mind-boggling complications and paperwork, this is only part of what government does. The real work of government is not only to defend the nation, but also to help people realize their full potential, so that our nation becomes stronger.

All of this is to say, I had a job to do in Imperial Valley. I knew the schools had good teachers. That wasn't the issue, as far as I could see. But I asked myself what I could do to encourage students to aspire to something more. Most of their parents worked in agriculture and had done so for generations. Most of the kids had never left the Valley in their lifetimes. And the message they received from the schools was that they had to temper their expectations of what was possible.

Every year, each congressional representative is allowed to appoint applicants to each of the three military academies. Each time I gave my presentation about these opportunities to gatherings of parents and teachers, they responded that they had been unaware that this program was open to anyone who qualified.

I approached each appointment in a true democratic process. We tracked the demographics so I knew how many women, blacks, Filipinos, Caucasians, and Hispanics had applied. I wanted my nominees to reflect the ethnic makeup of my district, so we visited each high school to recruit unrepresented populations. One year, we sent two Hispanic girls to the Air Force Academy—for the first time ever—from Imperial Valley.

Every other year, a congressman is also allowed to appoint a congressional page. When I announced this in a meeting with teachers and parents, I found that they weren't even aware the program existed. Evidently, my predecessor had simply appointed the children of his favorite growers.

One year, we sent one of the shyest girls I'd ever met to become a congressional page. She returned to the valley at the end of her assignment on Capitol Hill as an accomplished and poised young lady with big aspirations for her future. It was a fabulous investment in the community that I believe will pay off for her and her family and her community in the years to come.

At times, when people begin to understand the power of their unified voice, it can get a bit tricky. At a high school where I was speaking, the kids asked me about my job. I explained it to them by asking a question: "What do you want changed around here? What are some of the things you'd like to be different?"

It took just a couple of minutes for them to reach a consensus. One of them said, "We don't have a swimming pool." They told me that when they asked about a pool, they always got the same answer: "We don't have the money."

"Okay," I told them. "Here's what you do." They would need to do some research on the budget; they needed to identify which other schools had pools and find out what they spent on them. Then they would need to show up at a school board meeting and ask for a pool. They would need to find out when the school board was meeting and come prepared with placards and a petition. I told them that, if three hundred kids showed up, they had a good chance of being taken seriously.

The principal once again was not pleased with me. I had to explain to him that this was what was on the kids' minds. And since they wanted to know about my job and how I went about it, I had no other way to explain it to them except by an example.

Did they get that pool? Not just then. But for a brief moment, all of them experienced what it meant to be on the cusp of change. First, you have to know what you want so that you can articulate it and become its champion. Then you have to have the courage to organize. Then—and this is the most difficult step, the one that often thwarts even the most well-meaning people—you have to act.

It takes a commitment to organize. It takes energy and time and the determination to follow through on your intentions. Change takes time, and it only comes to those who work for it. But change is possible.

The Christmas Parade

By the time the 2004 House election cycle had begun, I had been organizing the valley for four years. It didn't surprise me when State Assemblyman Juan Vargas announced that he would be running against me for the Democratic nomination for the 51st Congressional District.

Vargas was already trying to become visible in the Valley, showing up at various events. I'd heard this from my constituents. The first time we showed up at the same event was late in 2003 at a Christmas parade in Calexico.

Now, Calexico in December is a little cooler than in the summer, but it's still hot. I can't tell you how many times I had visited this little town just to talk to folks. This parade was most likely Vargas' first visit to this 95 percent Hispanic community squeezed up against the border with Mexico.

We each sat in the back of a convertible, waving to the crowd as we paraded through downtown. As we passed the reviewing stand, the announcer introduced us over the PA. I'll never forget what happened when Vargas was introduced. He was in a car several places behind me, so I heard every word. When he was announced as the Democratic candidate for the 51st district, the crowd booed him!

I'm not exaggerating one bit. It was the worst reception I had ever heard. People in the crowd were screaming at him: "We have a congressman" and "Go home, loser." And those were the nicer things they said!

I was smiling inside. Not that I enjoyed seeing a man humiliated in public like that, but it validated what I believed: *People know your ideology by what you do for them.* That hot December day in Calexico, I wasn't Bob Filner, a Democratic liberal commie. I was Bob Filner, United States Congressman for the all the people of the 51st district of California.

Acting Locally: What Does Your Community Need?

Needless to say, I trounced Juan Vargas in the primaries. The people knew what I stood for, and that was why they voted for me. And they continued to do so until I resigned to become Mayor of San Diego, ten years later.

PHOTOGRAPHS

Bob's "mugshot" after his arrest on June 16, 1961 in Jackson, Mississippi as a Freedom Rider.

TRUMPING TRUMP

Bob works personally to clean up graffiti in his City Council neighborhoods.

Photographs

As a City Councilman, Bob "unveils" STOP signs that residents wanted for years to protect the safety of their children on the way to school.

Bob spends time with students in his Congressional district.

Bob pickets for job creation with his supporters in San Diego.

Bob introduces his longtime friend, Atlanta Congressman John Lewis, to San Diego. He first met Lewis, civil rights icon and "conscience of the Congress," in 1961 in the Mississippi State Penitentiary, where both were imprisoned as Freedom Riders.

Photographs

Bob marches with his good friend, the Rev. Jesse Jackson.

Bob greets Dolores Huerta, civil rights and labor hero, and co-founder with Cesar Chavez of the United Farm Workers. She coined the phrase, "si se puede."

Bob welcomes to San Diego, Ethel Kennedy, widow of Robert F. Kennedy.

Bob worked closely with Speaker of the House, Nancy Pelosi (D-CA).

Photographs

Bob was a close ally of Hillary Clinton, during her years in the White House and Senate and as a Presidential candidate.

Bob watches President Bill Clinton sign an important education bill while in San Diego. Also observing are Hillary Clinton and Secretary of Education, Richard Riley.

Bob tours the Olympic Training Center in his Congressional district with President Bill Clinton.

President Barack Obama welcomes Bob to the East Room of the White House.

During a tribute to honor Bob's thirty years of public service, his supporters sang "This Bob is Your Bob" to the tune of Woody Guthrie's, "This Land is our Land."

SIX

Fixing the Environment
Can Also Fix the Economy

Every nation must now develop an overriding loyalty to mankind as a whole in order to preserve the best in their individual societies.
                                    —Martin Luther King, Jr.

The Progressive Agenda: Climate Change

Our cities must get to zero carbon emissions if we are to survive.

There is no more time to waste arguing over climate change. We no longer need to debate what is taking place in front of our faces. Weather patterns all over the globe are changing and local patterns are in obvious turmoil. Storms and droughts are becoming more severe and prolonged. The

Arctic ice cap is melting, glaciers are disappearing, and sea levels are gradually rising.

The Natural Defense Resource Council reports[5] that the oceans have risen four to eight inches over the last century, and more changes are on the way. These changes are measurable and documented. And these new weather patterns are the direct result of man-made carbon emissions.

Preparing our cities for the full effects of global warming is not an option; it's an imperative. Cities across our nation are going to bear the brunt of the economic shift caused by climate change. The choices before us are simple: we must embrace this change or be swallowed by it.

One of the myths circulating in conservative circles is that anyone who buys into global warming as a man-made phenomenon is bent on destroying the economy as we know it today. In their minds, global warming is a devious plot (according to Trump, it's a plot by China) that will do two things: it will usher in a slow-growth economy that will phase out the high-paying industrial jobs that serve as the backbone of the blue-collar middle class, and it will increase the power of the liberal "bureaucracy." Not only will jobs be lost, they believe—but families will be destroyed by long-term unemployment. Major industries such as coal mining will be shut down. The ripple effect will reverberate throughout our economy, devastating related industries. The ramifications for our cities will be catastrophic.

The only myth here is that this is a plot laid down by progressives. It is not. The world we live in *is* changing

---

5. See www.nrdc.org/globalwarming/fcons/fcons4-asp.

environmentally and economically, whether we like it or not. On the economic front, our nation is in the midst of a radical technology transition that will continue to reshape our cities.

Think of Detroit. When the automotive industry went through a severe contraction of its manufacturing capacity, the change brought havoc to hundreds of smaller businesses that supplied the auto factories with parts and services. Whole neighborhoods were abandoned, and eventually, Detroit was forced into bankruptcy—the largest municipal bankruptcy in our nation's history.

Detroit was a casualty of the economic shift in consumer demand for large, gas-guzzling vehicles. Foreign competition with new technology and manufacturing processes drove Detroit automakers to become more cost-efficient and quality conscious. Mass layoffs resulted. Epidemic unemployment that became systemic and permanent turned the once prosperous city into a shell of its former self. Detroit took the full force of the harshest blow our capitalist system could have dealt it.

This type of shift from one technology to another—particularly in the energy we use to power our homes and businesses and cars—will have a significant impact on our cities. This type of economic chaos is going to sweep aside older industries far and wide. Changes in climatic conditions will increase the urgency of this transition. The skyrocketing cost of homes, food, utilities, and city services will further squeeze middle- and lower-income neighborhoods that are currently struggling just to make ends meet. This could turn sections of cities into neighborhoods filled with hopelessness, much as the economic shift did to Detroit.

That's why I believe getting our cities to zero carbon emissions is not an option, it's an imperative. And if we as political leaders plan for it, our communities won't have to endure the painful experience of the Midwestern towns now dubbed the "rust belt." I believe we can maintain the quality of life we are used to while easing into the new economy, because that economy is rising around us—whether we want to accept it or not.

In my mind, the great question is, how do we embrace this change—which futurists like Jeremy Rifkin call the Third Industrial Revolution—without causing the economic free-fall that Detroit experienced? Can we make decisions that benefit our quality of life by reducing environmental pollution while creating new, well-paying jobs that will bring economic vitality to our communities? I believe we can, because a revolution is taking place in our cities—the Green Revolution.

This is why the myth of a progressive plot to kill jobs is just that—a myth. We must and can be pro-growth *and* pro-environment, because this is the only way our cities can increase economic opportunity for everyone without destroying the environment ... and our quality of life along with it.

Climate Change: San Diego

I came into office as the first Democratic mayor of San Diego in twenty-five years with a long list of things I wanted to accomplish. At the top of this list was an ambitious plan to solarize all the city's public buildings. We have one of the sunniest climates in the country, and my discussions with solar companies led me to believe solarization was not only doable, but cost-effective.

My plan consisted of creating energy-generating hubs within each community. We would solarize a police department building, a library, the city hall, and other city buildings. The excess power we didn't need for city use would be fed into the surrounding community. I was very serious about this proposal because it fit neatly into the two main elements of my plans for the city. First, the proposal was pro-environment—and I intended to do everything within my power to lower the carbon footprint of the city's operations and then expand these programs into the community, to reduce and eventually eliminate all carbon emissions. This was a long-term goal that would also require us to rethink all energy use and public transportation in the city. It was my long-term goal for San Diego to become the first zero-carbon-emission city in America.

I also wanted to be known as the Job-Growth Mayor. From what I'd read, the green energy technologies would bring jobs to the city. This is the same conclusion Jeremy Rifkin came to in his exhaustive study of the renewable technology's impact on the American economy in his book, *The Third Industrial Revolution*. There were simply too many experts and statistics confirming that a new trend was already transforming our lives. I wanted San Diego to be ahead of the curve, not behind it.

For instance, one study by the Environmental and Energy Study Institute (EESI) in 2013 calculated there were 3.4 million green jobs in the U.S. at the end of 2011. These jobs were spread over several key industries that are continuing to experience growth. The construction industry alone represents a significant opportunity. The consulting firm McKinsey projected that between 2009 and 2020, an additional 600,000 to 900,000 construction jobs will be needed to retrofit buildings with new energy technologies.[6]

Solar, wind, and waste-to-energy projects are viable technologies for a city the size of San Diego, and they will all create new jobs and business opportunities. If older industries that use dirty-energy-hungry technologies were forced to leave the city limits, they would quickly be replaced with companies that benefited the community in multiple ways. Clean businesses deliver not only jobs, but also clean air to the communities and neighborhoods they are based in. This means healthier kids, healthier moms and dads, fewer missed sick days from school and work, and a better overall quality of life.

For me, solarizing city buildings was a jumping-off point for both job creation and reducing the city's carbon footprint. And even more important, it would convince the naysayers that this strategy of incorporating new technologies into city life on a large scale was not only feasible, but also cost-effective. I knew it would work.

After I had proposed the idea, I read Rifkin's book, *The Third Industrial Revolution*. His thesis is more radical and comprehensive than my proposal to only solarize city buildings. He saw renewable energy bringing an economic renaissance to communities across the world over a forty-year span in the form of a new distribution infrastructure, primarily a bidirectional smart grid integrated with the Internet that

---

6. Environmental and Energy Science Institute, "Fact Sheet: Jobs in Renewable Energy and Energy Efficiency," 2014, www.eesi.org/papers/view/fact-sheet-jobs-in-renewable-energy-and-energy-efficiency-2014.

would allow for the free flow of information and energy generated by multiple sources.

He believes what's missing in the attempt to bring more people on board with the energy revolution is a compelling narrative. His story begins with an observation that great economic transformations have occurred throughout history "when new communications technologies converge with new energy technologies."[7]

Advanced communications devices have allowed us to take on more complicated and sophisticated tasks because of the way in which energy is now available to us, according to Rifkin. This happened in the first Industrial Revolution, when steam power was first applied to the industrial printing press. The Second Industrial Revolution began with electrical communication and the oil-powered internal combustion engine.

The Third Industrial Revolution, Rifkin says, will be ushered in with Internet communications technologies and renewable energies. The modern infrastructure that develops out of this conjoining of communication and energy technologies will give rise to economic opportunities that never existed before the merger of the two.

Building the infrastructure alone will create jobs. But that's only the tip of the job iceberg. No one can doubt that the Internet has spawned some great businesses that never existed before its inception. These ideas at one time existed only in the imagination of a few science fiction writers. Now we can't imagine our lives without Facebook, Amazon, Netflix, Google,

---

7. Rifkin, *The Third Industrial Revolution: How Lateral Power is Transforming Energy, the Economy, and the World* New York: St. Martin's Press, 2011), 2.

and Twitter, just to name a few. These are big employers with outsized brands everyone is familiar with.

Many more regional and local businesses have been made possible by the instant communication and access to information the Internet affords us. Wind power and solar power companies and other green power generators will provide employment opportunities as they build out the new energy infrastructure, and these new sources of renewable, clean energy will make possible new ways for people to work and live.

It's not my place—or actually any politician's place—to say how smart people with initiative and drive will take advantage of these opportunities to build exciting and innovative businesses. We are only on the cusp of the green-energy revolution, and many jobs of the future haven't been dreamed of yet. But I believe they are right around the corner. Why shouldn't one of the major cities of the world, like San Diego, set the standard for what this new green city will look like?

Who could be against building such a future?

It's not coincidental that San Diego Gas and Electric (SDG&E) supported every candidate in the mayor's race except me. They didn't even talk to me until the day I took office, when I finally received a call from one of their vice presidents, who wanted to meet me for lunch. Lunches at expensive restaurants aren't my style, so I met with them in my office, where I felt more comfortable. They wanted to know about my plans to solarize city buildings, for which they offered tepid support.

It's the law in California that utilities have to purchase excess power generated by private users. They use a system called "net metering" to record how much energy is fed into the grid (the grid they control) by users who have their own solar energy-generation systems, creating a credit on users' bills against future use. Obviously, this is good for consumers who use their rooftops as mini-power plants.

But this law has put SDG&E in a difficult spot. California State law mandates that by 2020, renewable energy will account for 33 percent of all electricity generated in the state. It is true that utilities such as SDG&E are building out their own renewable energy projects. Solar power isn't a threat to the utilities' revenues if they own the generation plants. But even though they have major solar projects, the utility company will never make us what we need to be—a zero carbon city.

The same sunny days that work for them also work against them. As of this writing, fully 25 percent of all rooftop solar panels in the nation are found in SDG&E's service territory.[8] Then I came along and promised to solarize all the public buildings in the city once I became mayor.

Their executive management understood well the implications of championing the decentralizing of energy production. My idea put their old model of generating and selling electrons in jeopardy. Investors, stockholders, and executive management are putting tremendous pressure on the utilities to do everything possible to maintain their cushy and profitable monopoly status.

If the utilities are allowed to maintain their monopoly—which enables them to dictate how energy is created and sold

---

8. Lauren Sommer, "California Utilities and Solar Companies Battle Over Electricity Prices," November 24, 2014, https://ww2.KQED.org/science/2014/11/24.

and what rates to charge—the green energy revolution will progress more slowly. It's naïve to think that these monopolies will aggressively promote a technology that will further put their status at risk.

A new model of electricity management is emerging, called "distributed networks."[9] While this new model ultimately will reduce the utility companies' revenues, it will also provide them new business opportunities. But it's difficult for them to embrace these new opportunities if doing so requires them to let go of something they have controlled for the last hundred years.

That's why, in my thinking, power companies want to arrange things so that they control as much of the power generation as possible—even though the opportunity to create a truly decentralized, green city is right in front of us.

More Americans now live in cities than ever before, and buildings—commercial, industrial, public, and residential—account for close to 75 percent of all electricity used nationally.[10] If these same buildings were solarized, each would become an energy source and an energy distribution point, sharing power with other buildings while also serving as fueling stations for electric vehicles. For this to take place on the scale necessary for an entire metropolitan area to reach zero carbon emissions, we would need a revolutionary new energy grid.

---

9. See Rifkin, *Third Industrial Revolution*. The idea of a distributed network is that power generation becomes decentralized. The sources and power are owned by the users, not the centralized utility. The model works because the grid has become bidirectional moving electricity and information in both directions.
10. U.S. Energy Information Administration, http://www.eia.gov/.

The current, centrally-controlled grid one day will need to be transformed into an intelligent grid that connects many micro-grids, generating and selling back to a central manager. This new, smart grid will allow generators to share and communicate with one another as their need for power changes.

SDG&E is well aware of the future they are facing. At some point, they will become managers of a smart grid instead of owners and distributors of power. It's a new model that they eventually will need to embrace. But it remains to be seen whether they will voluntarily embrace the revolution in its nascent stages or be forced into changing by law and consumer demand.

I know what holds them back. It's the same thing that holds a lot of us back when faced with uncharted territory: fear of the unknown.

Climate Change: A Progressive Path

Let's put our finger on the biggest question of them all: who is going to pay for all of these changes? We are not talking about millions, but billions, and in some cases even more. Old technology will need to be retired. Workers who have spent a lifetime laboring in businesses that are being phased out will be laid off. Families will be affected in traumatic ways.

Many American workers will bear the costs of the change to smarter energy sources, and those costs will take the form of unemployment and loss of wages and pensions. The coal mining business alone will undergo major disruption, as will the coal-fired energy plants that are the gross polluters.

Just take the case of one major changeover in technology that is happening as I write this book—the San Onofre nuclear plant. The plant is half-owned by SDG&E. At full power, it generates over 2,000 megawatts of electricity for Southern California homes and businesses.

Because of a faulty design and manufacturing process, the plant started leaking radioactive steam from one of its brand-new steam generators. The same generator's rate-payers were charged a half a billion dollars on their utility bills for repair. When no one could come up with a permanent fix—or even an explanation for why the plant continued to leak—the Nuclear Regulatory Commission, prodded by adamant consumer watchdogs, recommended that the plant be shut down permanently.

It was probably the safe and prudent thing to do. But the utilities had sunk a lot of cash into this plant. How would they recoup their investment? And equally important, who would pay for new power sources to be built to replace the 2,000 megawatts of power once generated by the San Onofre plant? As usual, the utility found a way to maintain the status quo in the midst of what most businesses would deem a financial disaster.

The decommissioning will cost $4.4 billion. Rate-payers will pay $3.3 billion of that over the next ten years. But that doesn't include the cost of building four new plants to replace the power lost with the shuttering of San Onofre. With those costs included, the total hit to consumers will be $10.2 billion—or about $1,600 per electric meter in Southern California—over the next decade.

Why do I bring this up? Because the Public Utilities Commission in California approved this plan. Unless consumer forces rise up *en masse* to block this shuffling of costs onto consumers, Southern Californians will see these costs in their utility bills for the next decade.

Why does it cost so much? Because by law, the utilities are guaranteed a profit. So the first $3.3 billion assessed to rate-payers doesn't actually construct anything. Rather, it guarantees the owners' profit, as if the plant had stayed open. Call it what you want—a government handout or a fair profit—but it's set in law.[11]

We can question whether it's fair that consumers can be saddled with the majority of these costs while the utilities' stockholders are shielded from the most devastating financial effects of San Onofre's early and unexpected closure. But that is not the only issue we're facing.

This transition to clean energy will mean the disruption of old industries. Employees who have spent their careers in one occupation will suddenly find themselves without work they've been trained for. A similar process is unfolding right now in the coal industry.

One innovative idea for dealing with the severe disruption coming to our nation's outdated industries is called the "Just Transition Movement." In a recent *LA Times* article, labor activist Jonathan Tasini details how such a movement views job displacement that has occurred in the mining industry as a result of the diminished demand for coal.

---

11. Marc Lifsher, "Advocates Seek to Kill Deal that Sticks Ratepayers with San Onofre Costs," *Los Angeles Times*, April 8, 2015, http://www.latimes.com/business/la-fi-san-onofre-dispute-20150419-story.html.

"The problems start with the emphasis on retraining," Tasini states.[12] Retraining has proven to have uneven results in replacing jobs of the same pay scale, leaving workers to take lesser-paying jobs—or worse yet, no jobs at all. This disruption will destroy the middle-class wages and benefits these workers enjoyed.

A safety net has to be put in place to allow the retirement of people who are "modernized" out of their jobs. The costs will be enormous, but not out of line with what corporations are getting to save their own financial hides. If we can bail out the banks and guarantee the profits of utilities, then we can expend the resources to provide for the citizens of our nation who have worked hard in industries we no longer need. This is another solution to blunt Trump's backward policies.

Our city's leaders need to develop coherent plans that will bring us into the future without sacrificing the hard work of so many middle-class Americans. Major economic disruption is coming to the energy industry, changing how power is produced and distributed. The economic life of cities will be affected—for better and worse. New jobs will be created and old ones will be phased out.

We can't be naïve about the fact that there will be resistance to these substantial changes, but that should never slow us down or discourage us. Zero-carbon-emission cities are not a pipe dream if we know where we want to go and have a sense of what we need to do to get there.

---

12. Jonathan Tasini, "Op Ed: Who Should Pay the Price of Clean Energy?" *Los Angeles Times*, July 16, 2015, http://www.latimes.com/opinion/op-ed/la-oe-tasini-the-realistic-cost-of-ending-the-carbon-economy-20150716-story.html.

That is why, as mayor, I planned to bring Jeremy Rifkin to San Diego to tap into his vast knowledge, in order to implement the Third Industrial Revolution in San Diego on a grand scale. I believe there is a way to bring the green revolution into our cities in a way that creates more well-paying jobs than it displaces. But this won't be done without the cooperation of all the stakeholders in city life—citizens, businesses, utilities, and government.

This is not glassy-eyed idealism. Our future, the future of how our cities are organized, is being reimagined. It's going to take a commitment by those in the Progressive Movement to confront the status quo. We must take a stand against the vested interests who will resist revolutionary change as we seek a better way of life for everyone—one that has as much opportunity as it does promise.

SEVEN

Overcoming the Roadblocks to Change

Progress is a nice word. But change is the motivator. And change has its enemies.
—Robert F. Kennedy

One of the advantages of being a political realist is that it enables me to deal with situations, as they arise, in the most practical ways. It doesn't do my constituents any good for me to spend all my time in planning meetings or to perform endless studies just to issue reports and recommendations, or to fantasize about a future in which, somehow, people's problems will miraculously be solved.

I'm not criticizing those who engage in these functions—some of this is necessary and helpful. But I'm biased against those who are in positions to make a difference but nevertheless spend an inordinate amount of their time engaged in these tasks. Such people are typically paralyzed by their own analysis or too occupied denouncing those who have actual plans to get busy and implement solutions. In the end, they have little effect on the lives of those they are entrusted to serve.

I'm always concerned with ways to create meaningful change. I believe that change starts with working first on what is possible and practical. Making government more responsive to the individual is not as easy as it sounds. There are always roadblocks to helping deserving people get the assistance they need or the hand-up they deserve. Roadblocks stall progress. People who should be getting on with their lives are left in limbo.

Here is where the application of justice, equality, and opportunity breaks down. A just society requires that opportunities are open to *all* citizens, not just those with good connections. Overcoming these obstacles in order to make our society fair for the greatest number of our citizens will make us a stronger, more just nation.

One of the major roadblocks to substantive change and reform at every level of government—local, state, and federal—is the very institution originally founded to guarantee continuity and fairness in how laws and regulations are administered: the bureaucracy.

The Bureaucratic Shuffle

One day, I was on my way to a meeting in my San Diego congressional district. I stopped at a light and glanced over at the corner. Ten feet from me sat a man in a wheelchair dressed in a ragged jacket with military insignia. His wheelchair looked as if it were ready to fall apart.

I glanced at my watch. If I stopped, I would be late. I pulled around the corner, parked, and approached him. He was in bad shape. He'd been living on the street. The chair's seat was made out of wood that had rotted out from under him. I don't know how he sat in it all day. It looked beyond uncomfortable.

We talked a bit, and I learned that he was a veteran. I asked him why he hadn't gone to the VA to apply for a new chair and other benefits he was obviously eligible for. He told me the same sad story I'd heard so many times before: he had applied numerous times for help but had gotten buried in paperwork and excuses until he gave up trying.

I asked him if he wanted a new chair. He smirked, wondering how I was going to do that. He assured me that he had tried every way he could think of to get a new one from the VA, and he was certain it was a useless endeavor. It took a bit of convincing, but he finally agreed to get into my car and let me help him. I told him we were heading right over to the VA and I wouldn't leave until he got a new chair. He laughed heartily, with deep skepticism. But at this point, what did he have to lose by going with me?

I wheeled him up to the receptionist at the big VA hospital in San Diego. I told her I needed a new wheelchair for this man, and I needed one today. She rolled her eyes, the way people do when they're convinced you're out of your mind. She proceeded to tell me how impossible it would be for him to be seen immediately by anyone. There was paperwork to do.

Procedures to follow. He would have to make an appointment, and that would take time. The usual baloney.

My veteran friend heaved an I-told-you-so sigh of disgust.

I said I needed to speak to the hospital director, and I rattled off his name.

"That's impossible," she said. Now she was exasperated.

"You don't understand," I said, pulling out my business card. At the time, I was Chairman of the Veterans Affairs Committee, and the director knew me by name. "He'd be very upset if I left here without him seeing me."

She stared at my card for a long minute and then made the call. A little while later, I wheeled my new friend into the director's office, where I was met by his assistant. My friend was having a good time of it now, smiling all the way. I told the director's assistant what we needed. It wasn't long before someone showed up and wheeled him away.

Before I left the VA, he had a new chair ... along with a big smile plastered all over his face. He felt overwhelmed at the sudden attention after having been ignored for so long by so many.

Why did it take an extraordinary intervention to get results for one man in need of a new chair?

That haggard-looking veteran was more than a victim of his depressing circumstances. He had become a casualty of the very system that was designed, as a reward for his military service, to serve him. He had run up against a nameless, heartless bureaucracy.

I'm not singling out the receptionist as heartless or callous. I'm sure she was doing exactly what she had been told to do in these circumstances. But her actions were symptomatic of the major obstacle facing veterans seeking care—otherwise good people who wouldn't ignore the distress of dogs or cats will ignore human need when it doesn't conform to their set of guidelines.

This simple example appears to be a minor roadblock—telling someone who is in obvious and immediate need of help he has to make an appointment and fill out paperwork. Whether the receptionist knew that the appointment would only lead to more misery for this man, I can't say. But I do know she was following procedures perfectly and had no intention of doing her own assessment of the gravity of the situation ... nor did she have the authority to do so.

If she had taken a closer look and had seen through to the human need and potential tragedy right in front of her, she might have acted differently. At least she might have offered to call someone who could speak to his need directly.

That receptionist is only the tip of the bureaucratic force that has developed around every service provided in the sprawling Veterans Administration system. It has become an impenetrable labyrinth of layers of authority and processes, and it has confounded and defeated some good leaders and administrators. As a result, its inability to provide timely service in a number of areas has caused untold heartache for many of our veterans.

How is it possible for people to slip so easily into a bureaucratic mindset, in which the regulation is more important than the solution it was originally designed to effect?

When Training Works Against You

Bureaucracies grow out of the need for continuity in the administration of laws and regulations. At their best, they specialize in technical efficiency, speed, and accuracy. The strength of the bureaucracy is that each worker is trained to perform his or her task efficiently and impersonally, without preferring one person above another. Each worker adheres to the rules and codes set up to coordinate all the tasks necessary to fulfill their mission.

Because of this built-in rigidity, it's not difficult to understand how the system can ossify and become resistant to change. Robert Merton, in his study of how bureaucracies become dysfunctional, coined the phrase "trained incapacities."[13] Workers are trained to perform certain tasks using specific skills. They get so good at what they do that, when confronted with unexpected situations substantially different than what they've been trained for, they often make inappropriate choices. Over time, their special skills become a liability. They can't think outside the parameters set down for them. It's not efficient.

This explains the receptionist's response when I brought the needy veteran to her desk. Efficiency, reliability, and consistency become the key values of the organization. Following the rules and meeting deadlines with technical proficiency becomes more important than responding to a human being with a problem.

This is particularly acute after an election is held and new leaders take over. These new leaders begin to challenge

---

13. Robert K. Merton, "Bureaucratic Structure and Personality, "*Social Forces* 18, no. 4 (May 1940): 560–68.

the status quo, attempting to implement their own agenda. Bureaucrats who are resistant to change know they can just wait them out. Elected leaders can be in office four to eight years, but bureaucrats are in lifelong positions with seniority protected by civil service code. This is why most elected officials are unable to effect revolutionary change in how programs are implemented and services are provided.

When bureaucracies like the federal government grow to a massive size, they often turn Byzantine, like the Department of Veterans Affairs. The aims of the organization are often lost in their strict adherence to the rules. Leaders who want to enact true reforms must use force of character and sheer determination to succeed, or bureaucracy will defeat them.

I saw this up close with a very good man who was tapped by the president to turn the VA around. He ended up leaving in disgrace, having failed to achieve his goal of providing timely healthcare to needy veterans.

What does someone do who wants to make significant changes but is faced with a bureaucratic brick wall? I believe it's possible to make a difference, even in the face of entrenched opposition.

Make Yourself Visible

I first confronted bureaucratic thinking when I was elected to the San Diego School Board. As a board member, I wasn't expected to do more than attend meetings. They never thought any of the board members would roll up their sleeves and get involved with the details of the district, particularly how its operations and budgets were managed. It is tempting to simply leave the details to the professionals—to just show up and rubber-stamp the recommendations of staff. As you may have realized by now, that is not my style.

For one meeting, I asked the superintendent (whom I later replaced) and his staff for documents related to pending decisions for the next meeting. A stack of papers—I'm not exaggerating—three feet high was delivered to my desk. I had a small office down the hall from the superintendent, right next to their conference room, where I would sit and read. Of course, I read all the documents.

I always came to meetings prepared to ask the questions no one else was asking.

It shocked the heck out of them how I could come to a meeting so prepared. The more I had a grasp on the issues under consideration, the better the questions I was able to ask.

Often during board meetings, I was the only elected member to ask substantive questions. Many of the issues facing school boards and district officials are complex. They require special knowledge of the school operations, curriculum standards, budgets, and more. Decisions made in these board meetings affect the lives of thousands of children across the entire city. My incessant questioning of proposals and constant requests for more details didn't go over well with the superintendent and his staff. They had their own ideas about what was good for the district.

In every meeting, I let it be known that I wanted a more accountable administration. Their way of stonewalling was to continue to inundate me with documents and formal proposals. I'm a voracious reader, so none of that intimidated me. But this is a typical bureaucrat's method of overcoming any opposition to their way of thinking. Asking for more information raises their hackles. So they do what they do best: generate more paper, more reports, and more proposals—far more than is necessary to evaluate the best choices for the district's children.

I also made myself visible in the community. I spoke any place they'd let me and wherever there was a crowd to listen. As I began to articulate my vision for the district—that I wanted to see it run both more efficiently and more humanely, and that I was open to ideas about how it could be operated better—people came forward with ideas and concerns.

I made myself visible to everyone I could, from the motor pool to the clerical staff and from purchasing to the executive staff. If you don't know what's going on beyond the boardroom and the lunchroom, how can you effect any change at all? I don't think it's possible. Soon, I began to get discreet calls, asking if I knew about specific contracts or how they were awarded.

I made myself visible at district schools. Now, there are 165 schools from kindergarten through twelfth grade in San Diego Unified School District. It was time-consuming, but my plan was to visit each one. I began to show my face around the district, introducing myself to principals and staff, and I asked questions about their schools, the kids, and the biggest challenges to the achievement of their goals.

I listened and took it all in. I asked everyone I met questions about their departments: what they did, how they did it, and what could be improved. I constantly asked for their ideas about how to make their schools better.

It never failed—before I left the school grounds, someone would approach me. They had ideas, problems, and issues that needed to be resolved and were being swept under the rug. I also discovered who the straight-shooters were and which administrators or staff were forward-thinking. I made myself easily available by phone and e-mail. This visibility unleashed whistleblowers who, after the truth surfaces, help strengthen accountability at every level of the bureaucracy.

It didn't take long before I had a sound grasp of the issues facing the district— issues that needed to be resolved in order to raise the quality of education. It was a lot of work, but after my tenure on the board, I believe we had one of the finest public school districts in the nation.

Making Bureaucrats Accountable to Those They Serve

It is a difficult task, but not an impossible one, to make bureaucracies of any size accountable for results. Administrators often operate as unaccountable forces that possess their own dynamic. I think, in many cases, they operate without any specific ideology except to protect themselves. Despite their stratified thinking, it's still possible to accomplish true reform. One lesson to take to heart is the cost of failure to rein in the bureaucracies that are so hardened to change that they will go to great lengths to resist innovators.

During my time on the Veterans Affairs Committee, the president appointed a very capable man to run the Department of Veterans Affairs: retired U.S. Army General Eric Shinseki. The complaints from veterans over shoddy healthcare services were voluminous, and they were growing, so the president stepped up and appointed a real leader. Shinseki was roundly praised as a man of honor who had a deep appreciation for veterans' experiences, having served two tours of combat duty in Vietnam, where he suffered a serious injury to his foot. He took over a deeply troubled department, one that already had a notorious backlog of claims from Iraq and Afghanistan veterans.

Shortly after he took over, I read a book on veteran suicides. One of the statistics in particular was deeply troubling to me. The author reported that more veterans of the Vietnam conflict died as a result of suicide than in combat. More than 55,000 Americans died in combat, but the casualty count more than doubled when self-inflicted deaths were included. This was an ongoing tragedy happening every day in cities across America. With some work, we passed a bill that required every VA hospital in the country to have a designated suicide coordinator who would implement a program of awareness and training in preventing suicides.

My vision of a suicide coordinator would be a mental healthcare professional such as a psychiatrist or a psychologist who specialized in these issues. They would have the authority to muster support within each hospital for prevention programs and oversee the implementation of programs to reduce the horrific rate of suicides. We came up with a plan to develop effective programs at all 153 VA facilities. The coordinators of these programs would provide comprehensive training for the non-clinical staff and oversee the integration of mental health services with primary care services.

I believed that, through this approach, we could work to destigmatize mental health issues. We also could identify the particularly vulnerable veterans and channel them into mental health programs. By doing this, we'd reduce unnecessary deaths in a vulnerable population.

After the law passed requiring these coordinators at each VA facility, Secretary Shinseki appeared before my committee. In his testimony, he assured me that suicide prevention programs would be established, and that he would personally oversee the effort. He was as shocked as I was at the statistics coming out of the department on suicides among veterans.

I remember reminding him to be careful about whom he assigned to implement this task, and asking him to personally follow up to see that this was completed. Months later, he reappeared before the committee. After my close questioning about the suicide coordinators, he assured me the policy had been implemented.

"Does each facility have a suicide coordinator?" I asked him.

"Yes, all of them."

"How do you know?"

"Because I gave the order. They have to do it."

"Eric, they'll go right around you. They'll do what they want. You have to follow up yourself. Have you called any of the hospitals yourself to see what's been done?"

He shook his head. Eric is a good man. He spent thirty-eight years in the U.S. Army. He is a man of great integrity

Overcoming the Roadblocks to Change

and loyalty. In his previous world, when he gave an order, underlings saluted and said, "Yes sir!" That was all the confirmation he needed to know his orders would be carried out. He couldn't imagine for a moment that his orders regarding this highly sensitive objective would be ignored or subverted in any way in the civilian world.

But I could. So I took it upon myself to make some calls. I went through the list of clinics and hospitals, asking to speak to the suicide coordinator. In several places, the operator could not figure out who or what I was asking for, because no such position existed. In several places, I was able to reach the coordinator, and they were exactly the type of person the law imagined would fill this important position.

The sad thing was that in the majority of places, non-clinical staff had been placed in these vital positions. Not only did they have no experience dealing with suicide prevention, but they had been assigned the position on a part-time basis, so their effectiveness was questionable. At times, while talking to one of these coordinators, I realized I was speaking to someone who simply didn't understand the issues.

During my travels over the next few weeks, I followed up to see if I could meet with any of these suicide coordinators. The more I investigated, the angrier I became. Despite Secretary Shinseki's assurances, it was obvious to me that the task had been completed by people who had taken cynicism and foot-dragging to a new level. I was saddened and angered at this obvious effort by the people under Secretary Shinseki's control who had purposely subverted his will. And as egregious as that was, I was more saddened that the rate of suicides did not abate.

During Secretary Shinseki's tenure, he made valiant attempts to rein in a bureaucracy that was riddled with people who had no intention of putting any effort in to reform a completely out-of-control system. Why is it so difficult for even a good leader to rein in a recalcitrant bureaucracy?

If providing good treatment to vets were an issue of resources, we might be able to understand some of the issues. But that's not the case. The VA system of hospitals and outpatient clinics is the largest healthcare provider in our nation. It's extremely well-funded. Just because it's government-run doesn't mean we should accept its shortcomings.

Secretary Shinseki failed to make the bureaucrats accountable for their actions and decisions. One way he could have done this would have been to sprinkle his own people throughout the system—people he trusted, who would have carried out his orders and broken through the log jam of poor decision-making that plagues the agency. He also might have explored the idea of local advising committees with some real power to investigate, guaranteeing accountability.

He also needed to hold people accountable by terminating non-performers. I'm well aware that these lifelong government employees are covered under strict civil service rules that dictate how and when they can be fired, but a department Secretary has significant powers at his disposal. In many cases, someone needed to be held accountable for not performing their job, and to be relieved of their position.

Yes, it takes time to work through the adjudication process designed to impede the arbitrary firing of employees. But any government employee, regardless of their seniority, can be removed for cause. In my thinking, anyone caught scamming a system designed to save lives gives you a good reason to clean house. Never be afraid to make an example by firing those responsible for bad decisions.

A few years after I had left Congress, Secretary Shinseki found himself in the middle of anther VA catastrophe when medical records were falsified to show vets were getting timely appointments when they actually were not. The calls for his resignation were too loud and too many for the president to ignore. In the end, once again, the bureaucrats got their way. I don't believe it had to be this way. A good manager can corral a recalcitrant group of bureaucrats, but it takes determination and a willingness to hold people accountable for the aims of the department.

Be Clear About the Next Step

I've always had a bias for action. As a congressman, I've attended more meetings to hear out constituents, mark up bills, and do the business of government than I could ever count. I've learned that very little comes from meetings unless there's a determination to take action as a result of what's been decided. Even if a final decision how to solve a problem hasn't been reached, the problem-solving process can be furthered in some way. That's why, as meetings in my office came to an end, I always looked the participants in the eyes and asked, "What's the next step? Where do we go from here? How can we move a solution forward?"

People understand solutions. If the Progressive Movement stands for anything, it puts the needs of people above the needs of the bureaucratic machine. It's more concerned with results than with procedures. The opportunity to improve the lives of those we serve is in front of us every day.

Pushing results also keeps those whose tendency is to hide behind their procedures and rules an incentive to keep in mind the aim of the organization they work for. This should be the constant aim of progressive leaders: to pressure the process-makers to remember those they serve.

One way to do this is to focus on action and on taking steps to solve problems. Keep asking at every opportunity, "So what's the next step?"

Don't Take on Too Much

I had a very busy first hundred days in office as mayor of San Diego. I had big plans for the city. One of my early decisions was to stop all contracts from being signed without my personal approval while I got a handle on city operations. My goal was to hire a purchasing director who would report directly to me. This director would oversee all the contracts and see to it they were issued fairly and properly.

In truth, the contract situation became a nightmare. Yes, it gave me the opportunity to review all the City business, but because I had so many projects underway, the City staff began complaining that I was slowing operations down.

In retrospect, the better way to have handled this would have been to hire my Director of Purchasing first, then authorize that person to review every contract. It's possible to take on so much responsibility that it reaches the saturation point, compromising your effectiveness. It's important not to take on too much bureaucratic responsibility yourself, but to delegate it to trustworthy people.

I'm still convinced that the only way to get a handle on the operations of any bureaucracy is to have your own people in place, both in executive positions and in key managerial positions. Choose positions that are highly visible and fill them with people who will have the power and character to carry out your agenda.

Bureaucracies were not created to perpetuate themselves. They were created to serve their citizen constituents by fair and reasonable implementation of the laws. It's up to the political leader to see that his aims are not defeated by bureaucracy, by inspiring those around him to believe that change is not only possible, but necessary.

EIGHT

Finding Common Ground with the Business Community

I believe that as long as there is plenty, poverty is evil. Government belongs wherever evil needs an adversary and there are people in distress.
—Robert F. Kennedy

My primary aim as a progressive politician is to promote social good. One of my goals has always been to encourage business-government partnerships to benefit the community. The mere fact that businesses provide products or services for a profit doesn't automatically pit their interests against those of the community. Businesses play a crucial role in the health of a city by providing jobs and income that create the lifeblood of the community.

Restaurants, cafés, cleaners, bookstores, repair shops, manufacturers, distributors, and other entities bring value to a community in other ways besides providing residents with income. They also provide health insurance and taxes to support city services, and they promote social stability in myriad ways. These small businesses possess a connection to the community that is difficult for big business to duplicate.

A full 95 percent of all businesses in San Diego, according to the city treasurer, have twelve employees or fewer.[14] This statistic is most likely similar in every major metropolitan area in our nation. These small businesses are often financed by savings and with the help of friends, and they need the support of local government to give them the opportunity for a smooth and cost-effective launch. The most important thing city leaders can do is make certain that regulations governing small businesses make sense.

The Progressive Agenda: Government Efficiency

Nothing solves the most pressing human problems like a steady paycheck. If red tape and bureaucratic requirements are cut to only what is essential, small businesses will employ more local residents.

Just because I'm a liberal Democrat doesn't mean I'm automatically in love with regulation. Excessive, redundant, and overlapping federal, state, and local ordinances can stymie the most determined entrepreneur. I believe that mutually beneficial regulation of all concerned parties—local government, business, and the community—is the only recipe for success and prosperity.

---

14. Keegan Kyle, "Fact Check: A City of Small Businesses," *Voice of San Diego*, January 2, 2012, http://www.voiceofsandiego.org/all-narratives/fact/fact-check-a-city-of-small-businesses/.

This is not a simple problem of one or two more hoops for small businesses to jump through before they can open their doors. Over-regulation costs the business owner significant money that could otherwise circulate in the economy. They are required to spend money they would otherwise spend on their employee benefits, improving their operations, or investing in new ventures.

The costs to businesses to comply with regulations just from the federal government are staggering: In 2012, businesses spent $2.028 trillion complying with federal government rules and regulations. That's 12 percent of our gross national product (GDP).[15]

These regulatory costs fall disproportionately on the shoulders of the small businesses. Their economy of size works against them, not allowing them to amortize the cost of compliance across a larger operation. Excessive regulation operates as a hidden tax that never shows up in a federal budget. Overlay federal regulations with those imposed by the state and by local municipalities, and the small businessperson is overburdened.

One of my mandates coming into the mayor's office was to cut duplicate regulations, so that small business could get up and running more quickly. As a progressive, I believe I should be out in front in seeing that government encourages growth by doing everything possible to slash needlessly duplicated regulations and ordinances.

---

15. W. Mark Crain and Nicole V. Crain, "The Cost of Federal Regulation to the U.S. Economy, Manufacturing and Small Business," *National Manufacturing Association*, 2014, http://www.nam.org/Data-and-Reports/Cost-of-Federal-Regulations/Federal-Regulation-Full-Study.pdf.

Environmental laws meant to protect large populations are vital to the integrity of our neighborhoods. But regulations meant for large business operations often don't make sense when they are applied to small businesses trying to stay alive in a competitive marketplace.

When I was a city councilman, a dentist came to me with a problem. A couple of times a year, he used a minute amount of a toxic substance in his office to custom-fabricate a certain type of dental appliance for his patients. I don't remember the exact amount, but it was miniscule. He showed me how he could handle the materials safely so as not to expose himself or anyone else to the toxin, and how he was able to address any environmental concerns.

Since he performed the task himself, he was certain of what he was doing. Still, OSHA required that if he used *any* amount of that particular substance, he would have to build a shower in case of an accident. Installing a shower was a significant expense he couldn't afford, and in this case, one he didn't need. Here is the case of regulation gone wild. I worked hard to obtain an exemption for him, but OSHA wouldn't budge. Although it was a particular financial burden on him, he had to build that shower if he wanted to keep those customers for his practice.

Another egregious example of regulation gone wild is the Americans with Disabilities Act (ADA) that applies to businesses. Every business in America, no matter how small, has to make accommodations for handicapped customers. This includes restroom access, specially marked parking slots, and wheelchair ramps.

I agree with every bit of this law, because it has given equal access to many Americans who use wheelchairs or have difficulty walking. But the law has been abused by unscrupulous lawyers who have made careers of filing frivolous lawsuits targeting small businesses, the mom-and-pop operations occupying older buildings where the owners have been slow to comply.

Now, I'm not saying those businesses shouldn't have to comply. But for ruthless opportunists to take advantage of a law designed to help people with disabilities by extracting fees from small businesses as "settlements" is unethical. It's another example of good laws taken to absurd conclusions. What are courts thinking when they award damages to these charlatans?

Instead of taking cash out of the pockets of these hard-working citizens, the courts should give them sixty to ninety days to comply (or possibly even longer, depending on what alterations have to be made). Money should never go to lining the pockets of attorneys and their malicious clients when it could be used to serve the larger handicapped population. I don't need an expensive study to understand how these and many other well-intentioned laws place an undue burden on small businesses.

My emphasis on reducing red tape doesn't mean that environmental regulations should be relaxed only for the sake of growth. It means that the regulations should make sense. There should be an intelligent application to each situation.

I believe it's the responsibility of every branch of city government to streamline their operations in order to make dealing with the public easier and simpler. It's vital to every city that the small entrepreneurs who risk their life savings to make their dreams come true are able to thrive and grow. I regret that I wasn't mayor long enough to make significant headway in cutting the mass of conflicting and unnecessary rules to help make this growth possible—but that doesn't mean it shouldn't still be done. The future health of our cities depends on a more responsive local government.

The Progressive Agenda: Ending Corporate Welfare

State and local governments often engage in economic giveaways that yield few benefits. Large corporations are good at finding tax and environmental exemptions from cities, under the guise of stimulating local investment that will generate sales-tax dollars to fill city coffers.

While creating new jobs benefits is important, and cities need sales tax revenue to operate, there are often strings attached to these exemptions that cause havoc in unintended ways. When a city allows a polluter or a low-wage retailer to set up operation, there is a hidden cost shift from the private employer to the public till. Someone has to pay for these giveaways, and the cost typically falls on the taxpayers.

The most egregious repercussions of these exemptions always seem to affect those with the weakest political voice. Working-class and impoverished neighborhoods often bear the brunt of low wages, inadequate health care, and pollution that results in diseases, disabilities, and a lowered standard of living.

Walmart, the nation's largest private employer, purposely keeps a significant number of its staff underemployed (working less than thirty hours per week), forcing those employees to apply for Medicaid. Instead of taking responsibility for their workers' healthcare, Walmart decides to shift the cost of providing health insurance for its part-time workers to the federal assistance programs. By doing so, it offloads a significant cost of doing business to the taxpayer.[16]

When the nation's largest private employer—which less than a decade ago, after much bad press and public outcry, began granting part-time workers healthcare—exploits an Obamacare loophole, it sets a national trend that could become impossible to stop.

Why would a community welcome a Walmart by granting them tax exemptions—which could otherwise be used to pay for better schools and infrastructure—to open a store in an impoverished area? Why welcome a company that pays the lowest wages in its industry and forces the majority of its employees onto welfare for their health insurance? This just further impoverishes the community the company ostensibly serves.

These retail discounters achieve lower prices by leveraging taxpayer benefits into their cost of doing business. Walmart's lower prices are only possible because they pay lower wages and offer few benefits. This is a form of corporate welfare that only entrenches the misery of struggling communities.

Another form of corporate welfare is exemptions from environmental laws in the name of saving jobs. An egregious case of corporate disregard for communities concerns Exide

---

16. Alice Hines, "Walmart's New Health Care Policy Shifts Burden to Medicaid, Obamacare," *Huffington Post*, December 1, 2012, www.huffingtonpost.com/2012/12/01/walmart-health-care-policy-medicaid-obamacare_n_2220152.html.

Technologies, a car battery-recycling plant in Vernon, California, a working-class suburb of Los Angeles. Exide has operated in the same location since 1922, when pollution regulation was not on most communities' radars and population density was far lower than it is today.

The plant melted and recycled 40,000 automobile lead-acid batteries every day for decades, poisoning the ground and air with lead, arsenic, cadmium, and other toxic metals. Battery acid leaked out into surrounding roads, contaminating ground water and the yards and homes in the neighborhood. According to the *Los Angeles Times*, hundreds of thousands of residents across a wide swath of East L.A. may have lead poisoning because of this pollution. The county has ordered Exide to pay for blood tests for residents of the affected areas.[17]

The community lodged health-related complaints for years before state and local authorities stepped in and finally closed the plant down. Even then, it took a huge community protest to force the hand of the state board responsible for regulating toxic emissions. The complaints of the neighborhood were ignored for years while a gross polluter was allowed to operate under a temporary permit. In order for Exide to obtain a permanent permit, they would have had to spend millions on new pollution controls. It's obvious that the losers in this case were the residents.

The company rushed into bankruptcy when the local prosecutor began talking about criminal charges against the managers responsible. The company threatened to liquidate

---

17. Jessica Garrison and Alan Zarembo, "Exide Plant Will Pay for Blood Tests for Residents," *Los Angeles Times*, September 12, 2013. http://articles.latimes.com/2013/sep/12/local/la-me-blood-lead-20130913.

if any of their executives were charged criminally. This would leave no funds to pay for the cleanup or to pay the ongoing costs of residents' healthcare needs.

Obviously, this is not the type of organization with which any community could forge a bond of mutual benefit. They had no connection to the community and didn't lift one finger to aid the people their business had poisoned … until they were forced to. These types of dirty operations need to be zoned out of the most vulnerable neighborhoods so that responsible businesses can be brought in.

When a business pollutes a neighborhood, it's very likely that the owners and managers don't live in that community. Why should they? They don't want to be exposed to the pollution. Certainly that was the case with Exide and its absentee owners, who didn't appear to care one bit about the health of those who lived around their factory.

Progressives must stand against all forms of corporate welfare. The businesses I seek out for local partnerships are ones that have some connection with the community. These businesses can be any size, but the business owners must understand the value of giving back to the community.

There are a variety of ways any business can benefit a community. First, they need to pay their full share of the cost of doing business in their community, which includes property taxes and healthcare for their employees. They can't give handouts through the front door to build up good will and then send their employees out the back door to the hospital at taxpayers' expense. That is not responsible, nor is it ethical.

The list of opportunities for business to participate in their communities is long. They can adopt a school. They can bring kids to their business for a day of shadowing and mentoring. They can set up regular visits to a school that needs mentors. Relationships like this put education in context for kids who often don't have much experience outside their neighborhoods.

Businesses also can bring resources and amenities to neighborhoods that have few resources of their own. What do these amenities look like? When I was on the San Diego School Board, I ran such a program. I successfully recruited local businesses to adopt twenty schools. Every employer has unique abilities. I gave them goals for the program, and they came up with a plan to develop relationships with the kids. Why not tap into the creative spirit of the people who are making their communities work?

During my time on the school board, I only scratched the surface of what relationships like this can do for kids across the city. It takes leadership to make these efforts work.

I believe most entrepreneurs want to give back. They want to find a way to be socially responsible, but they might not know the best avenues to pursue. It's the mayor's job to find ways to connect communities that don't often speak to each other. The rich human capital in our cities—and San Diego is no slouch in this department—can be deployed in more fruitful ways that will grow a more educated and prosperous community.

The Progressive Agenda: Community Partnerships

As a U.S. congressman representing some very isolated

communities in the deserts of Imperial Valley, I always made sure that, no matter what we built with federal aid, the public received some additional benefit. If the district was allocated money to build a new Border Patrol facility, I made sure that adjacent to it, we built a park.

The cities along the California-Mexico border had very little additional money for civic amenities simply because of the low taxable income and property values in the areas. I always found a way to fund dire community needs that were simply beyond local budgets. For one isolated community, I found $400,000 for an extensive sidewalk system so the children no longer had to slog through the mud walking to school, as they had been doing for years.

Cooperation in capital projects between federal, state, and local governments is the way our federal system works, and it can serve as a model. A similar relationship between business and community needs to be initiated early on, when businesses begin to pull permits for construction or during the developmental phase.

Instead of lining their pockets with corporate welfare, corporations need to seed the communities that surround them. What if, instead of trying to wrangle as many concessions as possible from local government, they brought something of value to the city? They could provide internships, job training, scholarships, sports programs, and community service projects to aid depressed communities. Each company has its own resources and specialties. They could sponsor homeless shelters, aid underprivileged children, or help with after-school athletic and arts programs. There are endless needs and opportunities.

Granted, some of this is already being done. And yes, the large, multi-national corporations always engage in some form of charity. But often, their efforts are disjointed and don't benefit the specific communities that surround them. If all politics is local, then so is aid to those who need it.

Local and state governments have more power than any other entities to negotiate corporate aid to the communities they serve. Because they have this ability, they have an ethical obligation to use it. Businesses on their own very seldom seek out the common ground of mutual benefit. Opportunities must be consistently presented to them to seed their futures for positive growth.

The Progressive Agenda: Corporate Accountability

At times, my commitment to fight corporate exploitation has brought me into direct conflict with powerful businesspeople. I don't seek out such dramatic conflicts, but I think it's wrong to back down from a confrontation if it will *change* something in a way that will help people.

I once threatened to have Jamie Dimon, CEO of J.P. Morgan/Chase, arrested for murder.

The economy was in full meltdown by mid-2008. According to the calls and letters streaming into my office, Chase was showing no mercy to active-duty soldiers and recent veteran homeowners who fell behind on their mortgages. These soldiers feared eviction, and many were facing homelessness. Our nation didn't need the shame of allowing more homeless vets to wander the streets of our cities, nor could we permit the suicide rate to rise even higher among soldiers and veterans.

I subpoenaed Chase executives to appear before my committee to explain their reckless actions in pushing so many struggling vets out of their homes. As the Chairman of the House Committee on Veterans' Affairs, I knew I had to get these people's attention if they were going to change course. With the economy showing no signs of improving any time soon, I knew the situation in the short term would only get worse.

Mr. Dimon didn't show up at the hearing, but one of his senior executives did. While answering my questions about their policies toward vets, she simply recited the corporate speak on "honoring contracts" and "fiduciary responsibilities," etc.—typical bean-counter talk that skirted the meat of the issue. They could very well have offered modifications if they wanted to.

I kept prodding her about putting together programs to offer some relief to vets. They could rework payment schedules or forgive certain fees, or even lower interest rates. They had many options to help their customers. What they needed was motivation. We went back and forth fruitlessly until I finally gave her an ultimatum.

"Did you know we have an epidemic of suicides among active-duty soldiers and veterans?"

"I can imagine," she said.

"If I hear of any vets who are evicted from their homes committing suicide," I told her, "I'm going to have Jamie Dimon arrested for murder."

The chamber went quiet. Dimon's VP stared at me open-mouthed, trying to determine whether I had the power to imprison one of the most powerful CEOs in the country. I didn't know how I would actually have him arrested, but I knew I could stir some response by making the threat.

"I doubt you could make something like that stick," she said.

"Try me." I said. "You have the power to change your policies. You can if you want to."

Two weeks later, Chase delivered to my desk a list of five programs that provided vets with real mortgage relief in a variety of ways. It was a wonderful result. None of these new policies stripped Chase of their ability to profit from these loans. I hadn't forced them to give their services away. That wouldn't be American. Instead, they found ways to modify their terms to meet the needs of a vulnerable population. They could do it, and they did do it.

I often reflect on this episode. Why did it take a dramatic threat to get them to act in a meaningful way? Why did it take threats of arrest before they would take into consideration the human cost of the financial crisis that they, the Wall Street bankers, had been instrumental in creating?

What if business and government could forge a working relationship that benefited the widest possible population? It shouldn't take coercion for those with power to do the right thing. Yet those who govern have to use every available resource to remind businesses of their duty to serve humanity as well as their stockholders.

Corporate Accountability: San Diego

One of the conundrums I proposed to solve after I became mayor was how to fund a new stadium for the city's beloved

Finding Common Ground with the Business Community

Chargers football team. The team has been the darling of San Diego since they came to the city in 1961, and they have played at Qualcomm stadium since it was built in the late 1960s.

There's no doubt that Qualcomm is an outdated venue compared to the modern sports palaces that have been built across the nation in recent years. The problem with building a new stadium was financing. Who would pay for it—the Chargers, the NFL, or the public? There was tremendous public pressure not to get sucked into pledging hundreds of millions in long-term debt to finance a for-profit business venture from which the city would see very little net benefit.

Not everyone sees public financing of sports venues as I do—as a fraud perpetrated on the taxpayer. Take Petco Park, the San Diego baseball stadium financed entirely by city bonds. The justification at the time was that it gentrified a crime-ridden area that was not providing any tax revenue to the city. But after San Diego subsidized the Padres' new stadium by offering them a sweetheart deal that only a fool would turn down, the San Francisco Giants found a way to finance *their* state-of-the-art downtown stadium entirely with private funds. Instead of drawing from the city's general fund, the Giants contribute significantly to it.

San Diego could have cut the same deal with the Padres, but they didn't. Instead, they transferred hotel tax—which would normally have gone into the general fund—to pay the bond payments for Petco Park.

Sports franchise owners are an elite group of billionaires who have been granted a unique monopoly by congressional fiat, and this monopoly has made them supremely wealthy.

They have acquired much of this wealth by using public funds to maximize their profits. It's a profit scheme that is little understood by the public because its details are often misrepresented in owner-friendly statements and predictions of the economic benefits the city will enjoy if public funds are invested in expensive sports stadiums.

All but three of the original thirty-two National Football League stadiums were built with public finds. The typical justification for this scam is that every dollar invested will come back to the city double and triple in sales-tax receipts from fans who frequent the stadium. This fabrication has been so widely reported and so often repeated that we have been lulled into believing it. I say "fabrication" because that's exactly what it is. This return on investment seldom happens, particularly for football and hockey.

A case in point is the City of Glendale, Arizona, which floated $312 million in public bonds to build a hockey arena that has become a black hole in the city budget, producing an annual deficit of close to $12 million.[18] This is a case of a bad investment that grew worse as the Arizona Coyotes sputtered in the standings.

Public deficits are not the main argument against this public subsidization of billionaires' business operations. Many of the stadiums make a profit, just not for the city. The usual justification is that it enriches the city with "new money" in

---

18. Pat Garofalo and Travis Waldron, "If You Build It, They Might Not Come: The Risky Economics of Sports Stadiums," *The Atlantic*, September 7, 2012, http://www.theatlantic.com/business/archive/2012/09/if-you-build-it-they-might-not-come-the-risky-economics-of-sports-stadiums/260900/.

the form of sales tax receipts from visitors drawn to the sports venue from outside the city. But many studies have debunked this lie; very little new money comes into the area. The bulk of ticket revenue, concessions, parking fees, and restaurant tabs designated as "new money" is actually entertainment dollars that would have been spent by the locals even if no stadium had been built. Economists who have studied this call it the *substitution effect*. Instead of spending money at the movie theater down the street, sports fans spend their entertainment dollars attending the game.

This also applies to job creation. Jobs created by the sports venue are "substitutions" for jobs taken from some other sector of the local economy.[19]

What do the sports venues do for the owners? Despite the fact that these owners are some of the richest men in America, they continue to get richer at public expense as soon as the new stadiums open. The net value of a sports franchise increases anywhere from 30 to 50 percent after they begin operating from a new stadium. These same proud capitalists make much of the fact they built empires with their own hard work and acumen, and their willingness to put their capital at risk in business ventures. Yet they think nothing of using monopolistic powers, granted to them by federal law exempting sports franchises from anti-trust laws, to bully the public into financing the expansion of their wallets.

So now we get back to the Chargers, San Diego's beloved football team. With all this in mind, I approached

---

19. Christopher Diedrich, "Homefield Economics: The Public Financing of Stadiums," *Policy Matters* 4, no. 2(Spring 2007): 22–27.

the ownership of the Chargers with a juicy offer. I proposed that, since theirs was a profit-seeking operation—and since the city had the ability to issue the bonds and create the taxing authority to realize their dreams for a state-of-the-art stadium in the heart of the city that would make them the envy of the league—they would appreciate a solution that wouldn't cost them a penny.

Believe me, I had their attention.

I proposed that the city would bear all the costs of the stadium. We would issue the bonds, collect the taxes, pay the light bills, cut the grass—essentially do whatever needed to be done to make the stadium a world-class venue. All they had to do was provide our city an equity stake in the team so that we could share the increase in the net value of the club that would be created once they played in a new stadium. As mentioned above, a new stadium increases the value of a franchise by 25 to 50 percent. They would not have to make any payments to the city until the team was sold, which probably wouldn't happen for many years.

This realized equity reaped by the city could be used to build better schools and fund a modern public transportation network that would revitalize all parts of the city. It could be a real boon that would enable us to build a high-tech San Diego of the future without incurring more debt. Meanwhile, the Chargers would reap the profits to be had by playing in a new stadium, as many other teams were doing across America.

The owners laughed at me. First, they said it was against league rules. I reminded them that rules can be changed. Others had made this proposal before. Why not take a significant step toward becoming a partner in the growth of the city instead of just looking for handouts from the public till? There was more mirth in the room—this was something they weren't even prepared to consider.

On reflection, I can understand why. The city had handed the Padres a state-of-the-art stadium, footing the entire bill so they could have a downtown venue. After that, the Chargers brass saw no reason to give up part ownership, since other teams across the county didn't have to. Still, I was ready to stand behind it and make it happen if they had been willing to offer the city something besides a mountain of public debt.

Thanks to congressional exemptions from antitrust laws, the leagues can restrict the number of franchises. This gives teams that have developed a loyal local following leverage to force the public to finance stadiums. In other words, if San Diego didn't give the Chargers a new stadium, some other city would. It's a powerful threat, and one that has forced city after city across the nation to take on massive debt.

If my proposal to the Chargers sounded far-fetched, think about the executive to whom I was speaking: an entrepreneur who had probably entered many joint ventures to realize business goals as a builder. A publicly financed stadium is a joint venture in every sense of the word—yet there is no appetite to recognize the public's interest in profiting from the investment of tax money in a private venture. To some, *this* smacks of socialism—but I'd rather think of it as a good business deal, one that more cities should consider.

If I were still mayor, I would have organized a task force made up of the mayors of all the NFL, NBA, NHL, and MLB cities to develop effective responses to the extortion we all face from professional sports.

The Path Ahead

Business leaders have a lot to offer in leadership—an orientation toward success, a willingness to take risks, and most important, skills and expertise. It's in the business community's best interest for students to be well-prepared to contribute to their operations. Strong schools, mentorship programs, after-school programs, scholarships, academic support, and internships are just a few of the areas that could serve as common ground—the fertile soil in which to grow the skills and ambition the workforce needs in order to succeed.

Investment in human capital is as vital as the investment civic leaders make in building roads, bridges, and skyscrapers. One could argue that it's even more vital to invest in people than in infrastructure. Innovation, energy, skill, knowledge, and the will to develop a more just and prosperous society will rise from the soil of our efforts in ways that we cannot imagine. That's a progressive future from which we would all benefit.

NINE

Surviving as a Progressive in a Not-So-Progressive World

We shall overcome because the arc of the moral universe is long, but it bends toward justice.
—Dr. Martin Luther King, Jr.

The Progressive Agenda: Foreign Affairs

My re-election to Congress, term after term, defied the expectations of pundits and critics in both Washington and San Diego. I was consistently one of the most liberal members of the House, and I voted my conscience regularly on issues central to my values. Yet I continued to win re-election by wide margins in my conservative city.

One stand I took in Washington that I thought for certain would doom me at home was my vote against the war in Iraq.

I'm not a hawk, but neither am I automatically a dove when it comes to national defense. I reluctantly voted for going to war in Afghanistan because the destruction of the World Trade Center demanded a response of some sort. Yet I wasn't convinced that we needed an all-out war to accomplish that.

The run-up to the war vote was one of the few times I witnessed true bi-partisan resolve—no one wanted to be seen as weak in the face of such a direct threat. The problem is that an atmosphere of overwhelming patriotic fervor can cancel out rational thinking when it comes to making a decision.

I struggled with the idea going to war until the hour of the vote. I didn't see a declaration of war as a proportional response to the destruction of the Twin Towers.

The legislation authorizing the Afghanistan war was passed by a nearly unanimous Congress. There was a real euphoria that day. I get nervous when any type of war vote is taken in the clutches of an emotional response. The day of the vote, it was a stampede of "yeas" voiced with truly patriotic fervor.

The lone "nay" that day was from a Northern California progressive, my good friend Barbara Lee. She justified her vote by reminding us of the unanimous vote approving the war in Vietnam. I almost voted with her, and in hindsight, I should have. In the back of my mind was the political-military quagmire of another era.

Returning to my district in San Diego after the Afghanistan vote, I didn't run into one person who disagreed with my vote to go after al-Qaeda. San Diego has been a military town since the U.S. Navy first discovered its deep-water port a century ago. Sailors, Marines, and pilots are sewn into the warp and woof our city. Pride in our military and patriotism permeate every neighborhood. Voting "yea" to defend our nation against a madman made it easier for me to be a progressive in a conservative community.

What I expected—and what I believe many Americans expected—was that President Bush would prosecute the war with vigor and wipe out the extremists who had brought destruction and death to our shores. That's what he'd promised the nation when he stood on that pile of Twin Towers rubble. Like most Americans, I expected he would make good on his promise.

We hadn't been in Afghanistan even a year, chasing Osama bin Laden into the rat holes of the Hindu Kush Mountains, before President Bush demanded we declare war on Saddam Hussein as well.

Now this was a war of a completely different character. Yet another patriotic stampede was brewing to pass a unanimous resolution giving the president sweeping powers to prosecute a war under dubious circumstances. I knew the real issue was that our nation's oil companies wanted access to Iraq's significant oil reserves.

You didn't have to scratch too far below the surface of the President's reasoning to make that discovery. He and his oil-man vice president spoke as friends of his Texan oil buddies—and not, in my view, as the leaders of the free world trying to defeat international terrorism.

Then there was President Bush's misbegotten notion that we could export democracy in the same way that GM stamped out new Cadillacs. But nation-building isn't that easy.

Our national memory is often faulty. Only a decade and a half earlier, we had supported Saddam by sending him war materiel to fight Iran. Our strategy was to use Iraq as a buffer against an even more radical Iran. But when the world's oil supplies seemed to be in jeopardy, the entire Bush administration was tasked with trumping up enough evidence to justify a war. As difficult as that task appeared to be, Bush and his cronies accomplished it by cobbling together flimsy evidence that Saddam had nuclear weapons (or the capability to build them in the near future) to justify a pre-emptive war.

We went into a costly war based on innuendo, unreliable witnesses, circumstantial evidence, and outright lies. I was embarrassed for our nation.

As the rhetoric about Saddam's weapons of mass destruction mounted and the administration pulled out every stop to foment war, I remember sitting in my Capitol Hill office, reflecting on another time in our nation's history when this type of sham had been perpetuated on the American people.

Repeating the Mistakes of Vietnam

It was 1964, and supposedly a U.S. Navy ship had come under attack in the Gulf of Tonkin off the coast of Vietnam. After blustering about acts of aggression by North Vietnam, President Johnson asked for authority to go to war. The House vote was 416–0 for war.

What a disaster that war caused for our nation. It sent our economy into shambles, it warped our national psyche, and most important of all, it destroyed so many of our nation's young men. It was a war that accomplished little in terms of national security, but it set a whole generation of soldiers on the path of death. As I have mentioned, suicide is the most common cause of death among Vietnam veterans; more than the 55,000 who were killed in the war have taken their own lives. I don't need to say much more about what that war cost our nation.

As a member of the House Committee overseeing Veterans' Affairs, I can attest to the human toll which that despicable war still exacts on our vets. I've visited many VA hospitals where our Vietnam vets are treated. I've spoken at Veterans of Foreign Wars, Disabled American Veterans, American Legion, and Vietnam Veterans of America meetings across our nation. I've seen firsthand that war is a stain on the consciousness of our nation's veterans. For what? The war did very little, if anything, to make our nation more secure.

I didn't want to see another wave of injured soldiers who would need a lifetime of care because of nebulous and questionable fears of what could happen if we didn't take down another tyrant. If this war was about protecting America's access to significant oil reserves, as many of my colleagues believed, then a war to make the oilmen's fat wallets fatter would be immoral.

So I had some decisions to make. First, I was not going to let this vote go down like the Gulf of Tonkin resolution, for which the entire Congress fell into line like a bunch of blind sheep. I knew I could rally my fellow progressives and other like-minded House members to at least make a stand for what we knew was right. Second, I had to do it in a way that didn't alienate my constituents in my conservative district.

I was a progressive in a non-progressive world. I had a conscience and a constituency. How did I balance the two?

It never left my mind that I, like other House members, had to stand for re-election every two years. Now the drumbeats of war were loud and convincing. The nation was falling into line, according to the opinion polls. The majority of Americans believed what they'd been told—that the source of international terrorism was in Baghdad.

I was determined there would not be a replay of the Gulf of Tonkin resolution.

I joined Bernie Sanders and Dennis Kucinich in organizing an opposition vote. At the first meeting, only five members of Congress showed up! But we were convinced many other members shared our views.

We pointed out that the administration proposed to pay for the war with debt alone. They intended to borrow every penny of the trillion dollars needed to transport and equip an expeditionary force large enough to defeat a nation with one of the largest militaries in the world. What would this additional debt do to our economy? How could we be certain that Iraq's oil reserves would pay us back?

Then there was the question of what it would take to pacify an entire nation that had no historical experience with democratic institutions. The Army Chief of Staff (later Secretary of Veterans Affairs), General Eric Shinseki, testified before Congress that significantly more soldiers would be needed to pacify Iraq once the war was over—twice as many as the Secretary of Defense, Donald Rumsfeld, and his Deputy, Paul Wolfowitz, recommended. Rumsfeld and his colleagues were making bold predictions for victory based on careless military planning.

Rumsfeld himself, who supposedly had a superior handle on all matters related to war planning for the Bush administration, was interviewed by CBS's Steven Croft just before the vote. During this interview he said, on national television, "I can't tell you if the use of force in Iraq today will last five days, five weeks, or five months, but it won't last longer than that."

Hindsight shows that he and his advisors were dead wrong. But it was obvious to me then, as it is today, that he was deliberately misleading the country. He was slavishly following the Bush administration's line to its horrendous conclusions. Rumsfeld didn't know what it would require to win the war. He especially didn't understand what would be required in men and materiel to administer a nation of Iraq's size. Yet this was the man whose hands were firmly on the helm of our military.

Then there was the driving issue before all us: how were we going to catch Osama bin Laden—who had attacked us—if we were distracted by a war in another part of the world? As complex as Afghanistan was, Iraq was an even more difficult and hostile place to fight. Bin Laden's al-Qaeda network was a known, worldwide terrorist organization. We only had circumstantial evidence tying Iraq to international terrorism. It was a terrible mistake to divide our forces and attention at such a critical time, while we were attempting to defeat a known enemy.

We had many rational arguments against the war, but I knew the vote would not go our way. When the day came to vote in October 2002, the House passed the resolution for war, 296–133. I was very proud of those 133 members, almost one-third of the House, who stood up and weren't afraid to oppose an unjust and unnecessary war.

The Bush-Cheney juggernaut wanted regime change. Boy, did they get it. I wonder if anyone in the administration even knew the difference between a Shiite and a Sunni Muslim.

I'm sure they do now.

On my next visit home, I was concerned about how my constituents would receive me after such a visible stand against the war. Would they write me off as an unpatriotic liberal and send me packing in the next election?

Polls were reporting that many people considered a vote against unseating Saddam to be unpatriotic. Increasing numbers of Americans believed that Saddam supported international terrorist networks. The national media had picked up the Bush administration's propaganda and helped transform fiction into fact.

Unbelievably, Americans were becoming convinced Saddam Hussein was somehow implicated in the September 11 attacks. He *was* a despicable despot, but he wasn't the only one in the world, and there was no reason to believe that he was at all connected to Osama bin Laden. I had voted my conscience, and now I had to return home and face my constituents.

The Progressive Path: My Four Principles for Establishing Good Will—and Political Support

When I was in my district, I stayed busy. I went everywhere, attending meetings, giving speeches, and speaking with the media. After the Iraq vote, I made it a point to clarify, in all my presentations, why I didn't believe it was a just or necessary war. This was a war that would be fought solely on borrowed money, at the expense of our soldiers' lives, for dubious goals. Our national security wasn't directly threatened by Saddam any more than any other wacko dictator in the world was a significant threat to us.

When we go to war, we need clear reasons and a realistic plan for achieving our goals, or we're wasting the blood of our nation's youth, I said. This was a war that should not have been fought.

People listened.

What parent, spouse, child, or relative wants to see their loved ones put into harm's way for questionable reasons? The general sentiment in my district surprised me. The majority of the voters agreed with me. Any anxiety over how they would receive me soon passed.

My concern about my Iraq vote quickly dissipated. By 2002, I had been through five elections and I had spent my energies over the previous decade solving a wide range of problems in my district. I don't believe a congressman's job is to sit in his district office and wait for issues to find him.

I operated by four principles that I believe created a deep reservoir of good will in my district, so that my constituents were willing to trust my stand on national political issues. They gave me a pass when they didn't agree with me, knowing I always had their back when a local issue that affected them needed my muscle.

First, I always worked to frame local issues as non-partisan, never as "right" versus "left." Second, I gave special attention to "casework." Third, I was visible everywhere. It was said of me that wherever two or more people gathered, Filner would be there. Fourth, I never missed an opportunity for exposure in the media—always framing issues in a way that appealed to the press.

1. Getting Beyond 'Right' Versus 'Left'

My approach to problems transcended the typical liberal-conservative divide. In my very first City Council term, I joined forces with the most conservative member of the Council in order to seek legislative relief from an environmental requirement for an "upgraded" sewage treatment plant. We worked closely together to prove to the EPA that, given the ocean conditions, no significant environmental damage would result from continued use of the current sewage facilities.

When the legislation I sponsored passed (in my first year in Congress!), granting the waiver, it saved San Diego taxpayers nearly $6 billion dollars that otherwise would have had to be spent for a new plant! I was ecstatic, and so was the city government. The most liberal San Diegan had actually saved the taxpayers significant dollars!

My goal has always been to make San Diego a better place to live. It was this goal that often allowed me to reach beyond partisan politics and work with Republicans to effect substantive changes.

This transcends the stereotyping endemic to partisan politics. If the opposition labels me as a dyed-in-the-wool liberal who would never listen to their side, then they can divide voters and use wedge politics to win elections. The downside to this way of operating is that problems are less likely to be solved. Each side becomes hardened in its views, and little gets accomplished. We've seen this too often, and I was determined not to play to how people wanted to stereotype me.

This approach proved effective in my work on the House Committee for Veterans Affairs. I am against war, but I am for the vets. I visited hospitals and veterans' centers. I listened to their concerns. Every time I spoke at veteran organizations' national conventions, I received standing ovations before and after my speech. I brought the entire Democratic Party to the crucial political realization of the importance of caring for our vets.

I voiced my disgust at the shoddy health services provided to our veterans. I held committee meetings to investigate health and benefit issues, such as the effect of Agent Orange sprayed on soldiers during the Vietnam War. It took the Pentagon decades to admit to the deleterious effects of contact with that toxic defoliant. Meanwhile, our vets suffered debilitating symptoms with no compensation or treatment. Ameliorating suffering cannot be a conservative or liberal issue. Caring for human lives is the basis of our democratic values.

They can call me a liberal because I am. But they can never say I am anti-military, or that I am weak on veteran's concerns, or that I'm blind to issues of national defense—because I'm not.

So what am I? This question confused those who wanted to run against me or see me defeated by a politician who was more amenable to the status quo.

2. A Progressive Balance: Casework Versus Issues

Every day in my Congressional office, I received letters, faxes, e-mails, and phone calls on every conceivable issue. When these communications were expressing their opinions on the Iraq war or some other significant issue, I separated their letters into two piles—for and against.

Then there were the other letters: from a distraught constituent who needed a visa to visit her dying grandmother, or a request for help with veteran's benefits, or a Social Security problem. Not all of them were as dramatic as the lady who came into my office needing an organ transplant. The needs and requests were myriad, so I prioritized them and put my staff to work on them immediately.

I call it Filner's Casework Law: Your response from a congressman is inversely proportional to the national seriousness of the issue. There's not much I can do for someone who wants me to vote for a war I don't agree with. But if you have pothole on your street that needs fixing, I'll get right on it.

I personally worked to resolve all of the personal issues that came across my desk. Over the years, I had great success in helping people obtain visas, veterans' benefits, scholarships, medical benefits, and much more—even a heart transplant.

People remembered the things I'd done for them and their community, and they responded, term after term, by sending me back to Congress. They knew I worked hard for them in every way I could on local issues, so they cut me a lot of slack to vote my conscience on the big issues.

3. Maintaining Visibility in the Community

From my early days of political activity on the School Board, I made it a point to be seen. During my tenure on the Board, I visited all the schools in the city. I spoke at every high school and junior high graduation—and even some elementary school graduations. I've handed out diplomas to thousands of kids. I spoke at PTA meetings, soccer games, churches, synagogues, and literally anywhere citizens gathered to pursue their everyday activities.

I made myself available to speak to anyone who had a concern. I can't help everyone—it's impossible—but attempting to do so certainly gave me the pulse of my community.

Why do all this work? How else would I know how to make San Diego a better place to live! To do that, I needed to be re-elected. Parents knew me by name. Kids knew me. Love me or hate me, they knew who I was and how hard I worked for them.

4. Don't Miss Media Opportunities

I made sure I never missed an opportunity to get my message across. The media loves compelling stories in which problems are solved instead of divisions created. If you present reporters with story ideas framed in newsworthy ways, it makes their job easier.

When I went home after winning the vote on the treatment plant exemption, I made sure that the local media got the full story about how I worked together with the City

Council to solve a critical issue that could have affected the city's budget for the next twenty to thirty years.

I was an anomaly to the media—a liberal who was against spending money unnecessarily. People know when you're working for the community's best interest and not simply acting out a political agenda.

In my first re-election campaign, in 1994, feelings were still running high about the NAFTA treaty that had recently been passed. I was adamantly opposed to it. Not only did it drain local jobs, but I was convinced it would stimulate more illegal immigration instead of curtailing it, as proponents claimed.

I was ridiculed by local business people, who were convinced the trade agreement would be a boon to the city. They truly believed that shipping jobs off to Mexico—mainly manufacturing jobs—would help Mexicans yearning for a better life at home. I knew this was a pipe dream.

"NAFTA is a disasta" became my slogan. It only took a few years for the human toll of this trade agreement to become evident.

Shipped south along with American manufacturing jobs—which only a few decades before had served as the backbone of middle America—were hundreds of tons of inexpensive American corn. Corn and beans are the mainstay of the Mexican diet. When American corn costing 70 percent less than homegrown corn began showing up on grocery store shelves, the livelihoods of many Mexican farmers were destroyed.

Between three and four million rural farmers were affected. Many sold their plots and migrated north, hoping for higher-paying jobs. Since they only knew agricultural work but had little education, guess where they ended up?

You guessed it. Communities in Arizona, California, and the Midwest were inundated with cheap agricultural labor. The influx destroyed years of progress for low-wage American workers. Union jobs were lost. Wages on the low end were further depressed because American jobs were now offered at even lower wages.

Unreimbursed health care costs to local hospitals surged. The working poor couldn't afford to buy insurance, and these low-wage employers didn't offer it. So they got their health care in emergency rooms, which is the most expensive kind of health care.

What about the boom in trade in North America? Yes, there's been a significant trade increase. But who has profited from it? NAFTA benefited corporate leaders and their shareholders by lowering wages, reducing benefits, and skirting environmental laws. All of this has created more inequality and wage discrimination both across America and in Mexico. NAFTA eroded the middle class by whittling down their wages, and San Diego has taken the brunt of that wage deflation and job depletion.

Income inequality is not a chimera cooked up by economists and liberals. It's happening every day in the homes of the most vulnerable workers. It's fueled in part by international trade agreements that benefit the few at the expense of the many. I don't believe it's a liberal-versus-conservative issue when people work hard and can't make ends meet. It's a human problem.

Despite NAFTA, I worked hard to preserve jobs in San Diego. I spoke out against the paltry wages large employers paid. I did everything I could to help unions preserve jobs. People in my district knew where I stood on NAFTA because of how it affected their lives.

In 1994, during my first re-election campaign, the local power brokers convinced a successful Hispanic businesswoman to run against me. Since my district had a majority Hispanic population, they expected her to waltz in and snap up the Congressional seat. She had plenty of appeal. She was fluent in Spanish, she dressed and spoke well, and she was very wealthy.

At our first debate, she decided to speak out on the "benefits" of NAFTA. I stifled a smile as I listened to her talk. She obviously understood the issue only from the perspective of the business people. To me, she didn't sound like she'd ever spent much time with her workers, trying to understand their concerns. She sounded like she was speaking to group of investors. Sure, she talked about jobs. But jobs where? In Mexico?

She mainly talked about how trade between our two countries had increased. But she was speaking to a working-class crowd. Even before I got up to speak, people were booing her. Actually booing!

I made sure the local media made a big deal of the audience's response. This is one way to create positive visibility that reaches across district lines.

As it turned out, rather than being difficult, that was one of my easiest re-elections.

A Progressive Reminder: Individuals Count!

Not too long ago, I was jogging down the street in Los Angeles and a young fellow passed me on his bicycle—then braked suddenly. "Aren't you Bob Filner?" he yelled out. I stopped to ask him how he knew me—especially so far from home.

"What do you mean, how do I know you? You gave me both my elementary *and* high school diplomas." He was now in his early thirties, and an architect. We had a nice chat before he biked off.

Jogging away, I had to chuckle. He never asked me if I was liberal or conservative, or how I'd voted on the Iraq war or any other issue. He just remembered that I'd taken the time to honor his school achievements.

In some small way, he considered me a part of what he'd accomplished. He was proud when he told me he was now practicing his profession and doing well. And I was proud of him.

This is what America is all about: people taking advantage of the opportunities in front of them. This young man did that. And thousands of others from schools in my district have done the same. Who knows how my showing up and handing them a diploma and saying a kind word might have pushed them a little harder?

Don't think for one minute that being visible is all about self-promotion. If that's why you're doing it, then people will know. But if you're really serving by recognizing the needs and accomplishments of others, people will know that, too.

And they will remember.

I believe that the voters' memory of all the effort I put in on the homefront allowed me to survive for ten terms as a progressive legislator in a very conservative environment.

TEN

A Note on Language ... and Law
or
'Through the Eyes of a Newt:' Reclaiming Our Language

"The question," said Alice, "is whether you can make words mean so many different things."
—Lewis Carroll

But if thought corrupts language, language can also corrupt thought.
—George Orwell

Without language, we cannot communicate. And through a systematic effort in the 1980s and 1990s, from Reagan to Gingrich, from William Buckley to William Safire, the progressive vocabulary has been discredited and demonized. McCarthyism destroyed people and ideas; Gingrich-ism destroyed language.[20] They stole our vocabulary—and progressives were rendered mute.

---

20. In *1984*, George Orwell wrote: "The Revolution will be complete when the language is perfect."

Words that for decades conveyed a progressive message, an agenda, or a program were completely changed in meaning and utterly discredited: "liberal," "welfare," "taxes," "debt," "deficit," "poverty," "bureaucrats," "regulations," "immigrant," "peace," "labor unions," "food stamps," "voter fraud," "United Nations," the "public," "intellectual," "Hollywood," "science," and the very "government" itself.

New, dramatic phrases were created to frame issues in a conservative image: "environmental wackos," "feminazis," "death tax," "Right to Work," and "pro-life"[21]. Symbols of patriotism and American values—such as the flag and the Bill of Rights—and even God Herself[22] were expropriated by conservatives and given their own special meaning. The terror of War (well before the war *on* terror) was ***defined*** as patriotic!

Can it be more clear? We cannot move forward in any meaningful way until and unless we reclaim our language!

What precisely happened to our words?

"Poverty" is no longer an economic condition to be remedied—but a moral deficiency.

"Hollywood" is no longer an artistic and cultural incubator—but a hot bed of moral decay.

"Debt" is no longer a tactic for entrepreneurial leverage or even the pathway to the American dream of car and home ownership—but a moral disease.

The "deficit" is no longer an investment in infrastructure and people—but a moral crime.

---

21. Newt even turned "midnight basketball" into a Commie plot!
22. *Separation* of Church and State was designed by the Framers to *preserve* religion, for God's sake!

"Voter fraud" is no longer a simple crime—but denotes votes by minority groups for Democratic candidates.

"Food stamps" and "welfare" are no longer a means to prevent hunger and poverty in the richest nation in the world—but a moral abscess on the body politic.

"Immigrants" are no longer a source of invigorated national strength—but the explanation for *all* our problems.

"Peace" is no longer the universally-sought hope for all mankind—but the result of weakness and appeasement.

The "United Nations" is no longer the major vehicle toward world peace—but a mechanism for condemning American exceptionalism.

"Taxes" are no longer, in Churchill's words, the price of democracy—but a tyranny imposed by "bureaucrats" (no longer professional and politically independent representatives of "government," but pointy-headed, stupid, mindless, lazy "public" employees—who live off the dole and are loyal only to their political patrons) to keep us enslaved.

"Science" is no longer the rational search for nature's secrets that has not only been the hallmark of but has revolutionized Western civilization—but a "liberal" plot to strengthen tyrannical "government" control over our lives.

"Regulations" are no longer an attempt to minimize negative or selfish economic impact on consumer and citizen—but, again, a "liberal" plot to strengthen Federal (read Communist) tyranny.

An "intellectual" is no longer one who can help artistically, historically, and creatively interpret our society—but a pointy-headed (different in pointyness than the "bureaucrat"?)

rationalizer of "science," "regulations," and "environmental wackos."

"Labor unions" are no longer the progressive institutions that gave us the eight-hour day, paid vacations, and safety in the workplace—but compulsory gulags that enslave hard-working Americans.

The noun "public" is no longer the vast majority of Americans. It describes either the good guys who watch Fox News or the bad guys (the 47 percent) who demand "entitlements" from the "government." The adjective "public" no longer means for the good of all, but applies to concepts and institutions which only cater to the 47 percent.

And, of course, "government" no longer allows us to do together what we could never accomplish separately—but is really a tyranny imposed by "liberals," "bureaucrats," "intellectuals," and "Hollywood."[23]

Interestingly enough, the only word they were unsuccessful in demonizing was "gay." At first, gay rights seemed to be another sure-fire wedge issue for Republicans. But public opinion has solidly shifted in support of (could this be true?) same-sex marriage. And it was the gay community itself, insisting on marching with "pride," that turned the tide. That success may say something about standing up proudly and confidently about one's status as a liberal, a bureaucrat, a scientist, or an immigrant!

---

23. The ultimate irony, of course, is that they eventually made "Newt" a dirty word, too—in spite of Gingrich being a Ph.D. in History and not bashful about rewriting history for his own benefit.

Going even further, conservatives turned "corporations" into "people" (and thus made campaign finance reform an attack on First Amendment rights); justified the "me-me" society as "natural" and "right;" and "cleansed" the language accordingly.

Alongside the Contract with America, for example, Gingrich renamed many House Committees in 1995: "Education and Labor" became "Education and the Workforce," "Public Works and Transportation" lost its public nature and became "Transportation and Infrastructure," "Natural Resources" was shortened to "Resources," and "Government Operations" was transformed into "Oversight and Government Reform." The Gingrich Revolution was one of vocabulary!

A final note on this "great heist of the 20th century:" "Regulations" or other dirty words are quite all right if they benefit the upper middle class. Inspection is fine for our dinner steaks. Interstate highways make our family vacations easier. And our trips to Europe certainly require a safe international air system. We're even okay with "socialized medicine" for our veterans. Just stop wasting our money on those food stamps!

So What is to be Done?

I cannot answer this question by myself. In any case, that is the job of the Democratic Party, the Progressive Caucus, Progressive think tanks, and political campaigns from the Presidency to the School Board. But it is a job that must be *explicitly* taken on—and the sooner the better.

I would like to offer some principles and examples to further the cause and spark discussion:

1. Stand up and be proud! If liberalism means that I'm for equal rights for all (and the end of poverty, more jobs, better health care)—then damn right I'm a liberal!

2. Go around them. As pro-veteran, we *are* patriotic. By advocating programs for expanded adoption, we *are* pro-life.

3. Co-opt them. Wear the flag lapel when marching against war. Attack special interest subsidies as "corporate *welfare*." Talk about an education or infrastructure *deficit*.

4. Agree wherever possible without giving up principle. I, too, stand against *stupid* regulations.

5. Redefine the concept in terms *everyone* understands. Government is how we do *together* what we cannot do *separately*.

6. Invent concepts and programs that are as creative as theirs. Medicare for all! It's the economy, stupid! Better Yale than jail. The one-percenters. Obscene oil (insurance, monopoly) "profits" are really a "tax" on the middle class. Banks too big to fail?

Let's get to work—and make words work *for* us!

A Note on Language ... and Law

Filner's 100 Laws of Politics

(Actually, here I present only a sample—look for the rest in my next book!)

Sometimes, politics is not what it seems—and many truths are purposely hidden. My "laws of politics" (some aimed directly at office holders, others at activists) must be understood by all Progressive politicians—and citizens.

As an historian of science, I know that every scientific law is eventually proven wrong. As a politician, I know that Filner's laws are *immutable*—they are true now and will be for all eternity!

1. **First and foremost: Ordinary citizens, working together, can change the world.**

   I was lucky to personally learn this at age eighteen. As one of the "Freedom Riders" in 1961, we braved violent mobs and prison torture—and brought down the laws and signs of legal segregation. We didn't eliminate racism in our society—but we changed American history!

2. **The response of an elected official to a constituent's communication is *inversely proportional* to the importance of the issue.**

   If your letter or e-mail or telephone call concerns a major, long-standing or current global or national issue, the office will just count the number on each side. She will probably already have a position—and might send you a form letter, depending on which side you are on. But if there's a pothole on your street, five staff members will be charged with getting it fixed promptly! The official has actually *done something* (instead of just talking) and get the votes of you, your family, and your neighbors—forever. And you will be part of a press conference praising her responsiveness to community concerns—and you'll be on three television stations!

3. **However you communicate with the above office holder, find a way to do it in public.**

   Your initial letter is a *private* communication— she can characterize her mail in any way she wants. But if you submit the letter to the letters-to-the-editor section of, not only your major newspaper, but every neighborhood and organization newsletter you can find, thousands of people will read your opinion—and you can bet the official is monitoring those publications. She *must* be responsive! And she listens to the radio too! Whatever you write or call—say it on a talk show!

4. **Be there.**

   This comes to me from former Member of Congress, Barney Frank (D-MA), Official Curmudgeon of the House of Representatives. Between votes of the legislative body, most officials go back to their offices and avoid "boring" debate on the floor. But the best way to get to know your colleagues is to hang around. Unfortunately, it took me a decade to understand this truth.

5. **Progressives must learn the principle of "creative tension."**

    This comes to me from Dr. Martin Luther King, Jr. He knew that change could not come unless people were forced to think about the *status quo*—to become uncomfortable (to experience *tension*) with things as they are. So King's tactics were designed to produce this tension. But without *creativity*, responses would be knee-jerk, hostile, and violent. Thus were developed non-violent acts of civil disobedience, such as sit-ins, freedom rides, marches, and mass meetings. These actions forced people to think about the morality of segregation.

6. **Politicians will work on *your* issue more aggressively when they are in *competition* with other politicians for credit and press attention.**

    Invite politicians from *every* level of government that represents your area (city, county, state, federal) *all together* to a community meeting on your issue. When they see each other and all their constituents, they will want to be the *first* to solve the issue and, of course, get voter and media credit.

COROLLARY A—Whenever two elected officials at the same level of government share the same media market, chaos will ensue.

The competition that we see in Law #6 will be even more bloody.

7. **It ain't over till it's over.**

   This comes to me from Yogi Berra. All Major League Baseball fans know that, in a 162-game season, you can't get too high when you win or too low when you lose. The next game(s) can change things quickly! So it is in politics: floor votes can reverse committee votes, and the Other Chamber can vote down or amend your legislation. In other words, never give up!

8. **Start worrying when someone in the Other Party addresses you with greater praise than "the Honorable gentleman".**

   It is *not good* when you are called "the esteemed and honorable" or "my good friend—and he *is* my good friend."

9. **Language means nothing—or everything.**

   This comes to me from George Orwell—apparently read by Republicans more intently than Democrats. War is Peace. A Bush-era bill to allow clear-cutting of forests was entitled "The American Forest Preservation Act!"

A Note on Language ... and Law

> **COROLLARY A. The title of legislation can be crucial.**
>
> My bill to equalize dentist and physician pay in the Veterans Administration was originally entitled "The VA Dental Equity Bill." It went nowhere—until I changed the title to "Put Your Money Where Your Mouth Is." Then it passed quickly—and unanimously!

10. **Rounding up also means rounding down.**

    For budget purposes, appropriations are rounded up to the next million: $4,657,000 becomes $5,000,000. So I asked myself, does that mean less than $500,000 is rounded *down*? Sure enough, I was able to get many $497,000 appropriations for my district—at *zero* cost to American taxpayers!

11. **You *can* filibuster the U.S. House of Representatives.**

    It's well-known that the filibuster is a tool reserved to the Senate. Strict time limits make that impossible in the House. But several times (you can't overdo it!), I introduced fifty amendments to a bill—and I got five minutes for each amendment. That gave me more than four hours on the floor! They called it a Filnerbuster.

12. **Gimmicks are not gimmicks.**

    Progressives, particularly, need to learn this law. We take legislation and debate very seriously—we don't want to trivialize ideas. But we need to learn how to *dramatize* our ideas for the public and the media. Newt Gingrich rode this law into the Speakership.

During debates on energy policy, I addressed the House with bread crumbs in my pocket—and threw them out to dramatize how the big energy companies were giving us mere crumbs. At a Veterans Affairs Committee hearing on illegal foreclosures by major banks on homes owned by active duty soldiers, I questioned executives of the Chase Bank. When I got unsatisfactory answers, I said that if it turned out that a soldier committed suicide because of a foreclosure, I would call for the indictment of CEO Jamie Dimon for "murder." With national headlines screaming that word, we never had such a rapid response to a hearing! Chase agreed to give the families affected their homes free and clear of *any* mortgage, to hire 10,000 veterans, and to lower by 2 percent the interest rate for mortgages to active duty troops and recent veterans! Was I overly dramatic to use the word "murder?" I don't think so.

13. **It is *never* good when your Party leader puts his or her arm around you or sits down beside you in the legislative chamber.**

    She wants either your money or your (legislative) soul.

14. **Don't be flattered when a senior member calls you "Mr. Chairman."**

This comes to me from legendary Congressman Mo Udall from Arizona. He observed there were so many committees, sub-committees, and task forces in Congress, he had an 85 percent chance of being correct that another Member was indeed a Chairman. Today, it simply means that he doesn't know your name!

15. Learn Einstein's "Theory of Relativity" and Heisenberg's "Uncertainty Principle."

Though these theories were developed to explain the physical world, they also help us to understand the world of politics.

> COROLLARY A. It's a fact—unless the other Party says so.
>
> COROLLARY B. It's only unethical if you're a member of the Minority Party.
>
> COROLLARY C. Bribery is illegal—unless it involves a Congress member. Then it's called a "campaign contribution."

16. Public officials sell out cheaply.

Lobbyists or wealthy donors may give several thousand dollars to a campaign. But whether it's a specific appropriation, a contract, or a regulatory ruling, its payback is *millions* of dollars.

> COROLLARY A. We Progressives say that the Republicans are bought and paid for. *(So are the Democrats.)*

17. It's not true until the elevator operator says so.

Rumors fly around the Capitol about the day or time of adjournment or how a particular vote will go. But since everyone will, at some time during the day, be in an elevator, only the operator can detect the truth.

18. Unless there's a photo—it didn't happen.

Your constituents and the press need the photo to prove you were there, whether it's for today's newspaper or tomorrow's memoirs. I have been known to "photo bomb" Presidents of the United States!

> **COROLLARY A. You are in bodily danger if you are standing between a politician and a President, foreign dignitary, or Hollywood celebrity.**

We should sell tickets of admission to such events, especially if more than one politician is in attendance—each one seeking a "photo op." Think of penalties in the NFL or NHL: clipping, false starts, chop blocks, roughing the passer, illegal use of hands, or unsportsmanlike conduct!

19. Tongues are more loose in the gym than in a bar.

It may be the only place in the Capitol where Rs and Ds talk freely to each other!

20. "Madame Speaker, this House is out of order."

The best response when you are addressing your colleagues with the world's most stirring speech and are ruled "out of order."

A Note on Language ... and Law

21. Start worrying when your meal companion says "it's on me."

Pay me now or pay me later.

22. There's always another room.

Every time I walked into a room of my colleagues for policy decisions, it seemed to me that the decision was already made—that this meeting was only a charade. As I moved up in seniority—from caucus member to the Leader's executive committee to a committee of all Chairpersons—I always wondered where the room was in which everything was decided. I never found it.

23. Have your own plane.

On "fact finding" trips abroad by Members of Congress, there is apt to be a lot of shopping. I once overheard a Venice shopkeeper tell a member's wife, who had purchased a large mirror of fine Venetian glass, that the item was too large to ship. The reply: "Don't worry, we have our own plane!"

24. When writing speeches, always add adjectives. When writing speeches, always eliminate adjectives.

Everything depends on your boss. When I worked for Senator Hubert Humphrey, there were never enough adverbs and adjectives to add. When I worked for straight-talking Congressman Don Fraser from the same state of Minnesota, I could just take a Humphrey speech—and cross out all the modifiers.

25. Copy everything before you throw it away.

This comes to me from a directive from one of my chiefs-of-staff to his staff to illustrate my obsession with saving and filing all paperwork.

26. Know where the kitchen is.

It is sometimes necessary to leave an event early—and might well be embarrassing if everyone saw your exit. Most events are in venues where there is an adjacent kitchen, which can provide an anonymous exit. Once, when there was no kitchen, I found an escape window in the bathroom! (My loyal staff member, following *his* Laws of Politics, waited for me outside the bathroom for several hours!)

27. There's always a back door.

An intern in my office, who was tasked to deliver a late press release to a television station, arrived there at 5:03 p.m.—and then returned to our office saying that the office closed at 5:00 p.m. and he couldn't leave the release. Of course, all TV stations have a back door—but this became a law about the necessity of being resourceful in order to complete an assignment.

A Note on Language ... and Law

28. Wherever two people gather, you need to be there.

As a candidate or an elected official, be visible. My constituents thought I had a couple of clones.

29. Know how to say "thank you" and "good morning" in twelve different languages.

Notwithstanding the views of Donald Trump, we are still a very diverse nation.

30. Never forget the three "Bs".

Be brief, Be personal—and Be gone.

CPSIA information can be obtained
at www.ICGtesting.com
Printed in the USA
FSHW011556250321
79793FS

9 780692 877166